MW01037422

The Word Embodied

Dear Connie,

    Happy Birthday, dear friend!
I hope you enjoy this book. I know
you treasure God's Word, so thought
you might find Fr Kavanaugh's
reflections helpful in breaking open
the Word. Art and I read it
most Sunday mornings before Mass.
It helps us enter the Mass more
prepared to listen. Sometimes it
is similar to the homily that day and
other times totally different. Enjoy!

                    Love,
                    Dianne

The Word Embodied

Meditations on the Sunday Scriptures
Cycle A

JOHN F. KAVANAUGH

ORBIS BOOKS

Maryknoll, New York 10545

The Catholic Foreign Mission Society of America (Maryknoll) recruits and trains people for overseas missionary service. Through Orbis Books, Maryknoll aims to foster the international dialogue that is essential to mission. The books published, however, reflect the opinions of their authors and are not meant to represent the official position of the society.

Library of Congress Cataloging-in-Publication Data

Kavanaugh, John F.
    The Word embodied : meditations on the Sunday Scriptures : cycle A /John F. Kavanaugh.
       p.   cm.
    ISBN 1-57075-198-6 (pbk.)
    1. Church year meditations.   2. Bible—Liturgical lessons, English—Meditations.   3. Catholic Church—Prayer-books and devotions—English.   I. Title.
    BX2170.C55K376   1998
    242'.3—dc21   98-20947
                                                            CIP

For the extended family,
dear aunts, uncles, cousins,
especially the children of my Uncle James Keaveney
of Galway, Ireland,
Kathleen, Tess, Margaret, and Seamus

Contents

vii

Preface

Our faith is nothing if it is not about the Embodied Word of God. This is Jesus, the Christ, who is flesh of our flesh and yet, we believe, in total union with the *Mysterium Tremendens et Fascinans*. Thus, our prayer as our preaching will always be pulled in two directions: more deeply into our humanity, more outside of us into the Wholly Other, our God.

The word of God that is our holy scripture is just as time-lodged and just as transcendent as the Word made flesh. We believe it is no mere human concoction, and yet it only exists by human mediation: a given time, a particular culture, a specific language. Yet it addresses all ages, all tribes, and every tongue.

Thus it is with all our encountering of God, all our glimpses at the face of Christ: human yet divine, commonplace yet awesome, ordinary yet irreplaceable, a concrete individual who gives body to the most unimaginable of mysteries.

My Jesuit community has been that to me, in all our diversity as well as our great common aspiration and longing. It has been the infirm of us, the old and wheelchair bound, who have most drawn me to speak of the Word in our Wednesday morning liturgies. And despite the pain I feel in seeing their diminishment, they have revealed to me joyful mysteries I had hitherto not known.

Saint Francis Xavier College Church, where I am privileged to serve as an assisting priest, also profoundly embodies the Word of God for all who worship or visit there. The architecture awesome, the music always lovely and lifting, it is the people who, especially at the testimony of communion, win your heart and help you understand how God might have fallen in love with us.

The great parade of university students, those I've instructed at Saint Louis University, those who have formed lay
communities of faith, service, and justice, and those who have
revealed wondrous faith, hope, and love in the Catholic
Student Center of Washington University, are Word made
flesh. They are so real, so concretely good. But they are utterly
inexplicable without the kind invasion of God in time.

Brothers and sisters in faith who have welcomed any priest
into their lives through the sheer gift of the sacraments will,
I'm confident, someday know how they have embodied the
Word of God in their love for their newborn babies, their
unguarded moments of repentance, their delight and courage
in marrying, their tenderness in dying, their mature commitment to conversion.

> The Word was made Flesh
> And dwelt among us
> And we have seen the Glory.

1. Seeing Daylight

Is. 2:1–5; Rom. 13:11–14; Mt. 24:37–44

"Now is the hour."

Symbols are rarely unambiguous. Even the image of the dove or the lion has its shadow. Water is life-giving, but it can take away your life just as surely. It may cleanse, but it is also treacherous. Fire is furious; fire is comforting. Clouds have silver linings. Countless images have their positive and negative faces.

So it is with night. Nights have starry skies that inspire philosophers like Kant and artists like van Gogh. The night brings rest and quiet. It signals not only endings, but expectancy.

But night, at least in Advent-time, has less ambiguity than most imagery. It is something to escape. Utter night, without the promise of morning, is deepest gloom. Endless night, without the glow of candle or star, is a void. Even ordinary and partial night is more scary than starry.

It is best we sleep in the dark. At night violent armies clash. Streets clatter with shouts and gunfire, sometimes even until the break of dawn. Debaucheries, betrayals, carousing are heard faintly in the distance. Nearby, once "the night is far spent," Paul phrases it, the stumbling home from wild desires sounds a city night's death-knell.

Sudden shadows that leap and loom trouble us at night far more than the tame shadows of daytime. If we are startled from a midnight sleep, we may feel a terror greater than at any other time: some gaping darkness, some unexpected anxiety, some uncovered dread. If we sleep again, our unconscious has

1

its say, unkempt, untrammeled, unmanageable in its better dreams, horrific in its nightmares.

Sadly, even in the day we often sleep-walk as we eat, drink, and parent, too often unknowing and unconcerned. When we do manage to stir ourselves to action, we routinely play out a strident score written by our conductor of night—the dark unconscious. Freud's find, the libido, stalks the world day and night for prey or power or pleasure. Our quarrels, jealousies, and wars are works of darkness, even though they haunt our days.

Darkness was the lifeless void of Genesis, the ninth ominous plague of Egypt foreshadowing its terrible tenth: the death of all firstborn.

Isaiah promised that the works of dark and sleep would all be changed in God's bright presence. "They shall beat their swords into plowshares and their spears into pruning hooks; one nation shall not raise the sword against another, nor shall they train for war again. . . . Come, let us walk in the light of the Lord." To see in the light of eternity is to change. If we knew as God knows, if we were "instructed in God's ways," if we walked in God's paths, not only would our nations disarm, we would tear down our more private defenses. We would never again make war against each other, against our very hearts.

The Fourth Gospel announced God as light in whom there is no darkness, the light that shines in human night, irradiating our world. It was light, the First Letter of John would teach, that opened the way to life and love.

Paul advises the Romans (they themselves knew their dreadful nights) to be conscious of the day. They are to live now what they want forever. Salvation is nigh, Paul says. Be awake. Walk with the armor of light.

The Ephesians were to be children of the day, awake and vigilant. "Wake from your sleep, rise from the dead, and Christ will shine on you."

Since we do not know the time when our lives stop or the earth melts, every day must be one of presence. Vigilance is for now. The watchful eye, the expectant heart, is for this moment. If we are sleep-walking our way through life, now is the time to "come to."

Advent. Enter. To "come to." To wake up. To enter life, here and today. Let God enter it all and now. And let us enter it all, even the darkness, now with God.

If we go into our lives and permit God to enter with us, then we shall see, even though it be night. Revelation—enlightenment—will come to us, not in shrouded nightmare, but upon a midnight clear. Then we shall no longer be the walking dead. And even though we walk through the valley of darkness, no evil shall we fear.

The clamor of the streets will be stilled, for it will be a silent night. The deceptions of the dark will be uncovered, for it will be a holy night. Night itself will be transformed, transfigured, when all is calm, when all is bright.

And we shall sing with Zechariah his canticle of illumination, a song of the life that is light.

> In the tender compassion of our God
> The dawn from on high shall break upon us
> To shine on those who dwell in darkness
> And the shadow of death,
> To guide our feet into the way of peace.

2. Entrance Rites

Is. 11:1–10; Rom. 15:4–9; Mt. 3:1–12

"Reform your lives."

In the Spiritual Exercises of St. Ignatius of Loyola, one of the more elaborate meditations is a study of the Incarnation. Ignatius has us imagine the Trinity gazing upon the world, desiring to save the human race. He paints a vast mural of persons, various in dress, actions, and color, "some in peace and others in war; some weeping and others laughing; some well, others ill; some being born and others dying."

But there is great blindness in humanity. People not only lose their way; they lose their souls as well. So Ignatius writes of the great entry. God, in the second person of the Trinity, chooses to be one of us. In an earthly village the Virgin gives herself in gratitude and trust.

The entry of God is not only portrayed as a religious experience by individual persons, it is also an invasion of history itself, a breaching of the geopolitical and social worlds of all humankind.

This global emphasis did not originate with Ignatius of Loyola. It is clear even from the prophetic utterances of Isaiah that the Messiah, upon whom the Spirit of the Lord would rest, was to be of vast importance, not only to Israel, but to the Gentile world as "a signal for the nations."

Isaiah tells us that the promised one, with the wisdom and understanding of God's Spirit, will judge the poor with justice and strike the ruthless and wicked. He will carry a peace to the world that transforms even the animals. Wolves will eat with lambs, leopards with kids. Lions will browse with calves, cows, and bears. Babies will play near cobras as if they were kindly neighbors. A little child will lead the entire earth, where "there shall be no harm or ruin."

Paul's Letter to the Romans reminds his readers that the advent of Christ into their lives will require a reform, as well, of their personal relationships. The mercy of God will enable them "to live in perfect harmony with one another according to the spirit of Christ Jesus." They are henceforth to accept each other in the same way that Christ accepted them. Therein, they will reveal the glory of God.

The reforming power of God's advent, finally, must penetrate our interior lives. This was the message of John the Baptizer. We may, like the Pharisees, go through the motions of baptism, but we are commanded to "give some evidence that you mean to reform." It is not enough to proclaim that we are saved. We must yield our entire being for purification by the Holy Spirit and fire.

Many Christians seem to have a problem with the total message of the Incarnation and Christ's advent. They tend to select some safe portion of their lives which they open to God while they slam shut all the others.

Some of us think we can get by with allowing God to enter our interior "prayer lives." We try to hold the reform to that. We resist the possibility that our relation to our families or friends could be transformed. We can't imagine that we would have to change our attitudes toward our enemies. And we certainly would not tolerate any challenge to our pet political suppositions or economic practices.

Others think their personal relationships can be transformed, but not their interior hearts or their external world. "I find God in my relationships and my friends. I don't need personal prayer, and I can't worry about the world." This attitude refuses to acknowledge that solitude and social justice are essential in our relationship to God.

Finally, some of us ardently believe in the social gospel. We want the world to be saved. We insist that the Democrats and Republicans be reformed. We demand that the church be changed and nations disarmed. But it rarely strikes us that we may be as unjust in our own relationships as the principalities and powers are in theirs. We can't imagine that we, in our own way, could be as narcissistic and self-centered as preening politicians and avaricious misers.

If we restrict the entry of God into our lives, we cannot help but limit the power of God's grace. When we wonder why our path of discipleship seems to lead nowhere, it may be because we have set up too many roadblocks.

The narratives of the Advent gospels, like Ignatius's meditation on the Incarnation, reach beyond nations out to the cosmos and down into the individual heart. The coming of

Christ is an event for the universe. It is an event for history and an event for each of us in our personal struggles and interpersonal relationships.

Our entry into Advent, like the entrance rite of every Eucharist, is most effective when it is most expansive. When our arms are fully open, we welcome God to embrace all of us, every part of us.

We Christians must be about the reform of our nations as well as of our church. Lord, have mercy.

We must be about reconciliation with our families and our friends. Christ, have mercy.

And we must be about the acknowledgment of our own failure. Lord, have mercy.

What does such penitence lead to? Not sadness, but "glory to God in the highest, and peace to God's people on earth."

3. Waiting

Is. 35:1–6, 10; Jas. 5:7–10; Mt. 11:2–11

"Sorrow and mourning will flee."

The days of Advent wore on slowly for me last year. It was not like waiting for some promise. I was dreading a disaster.

My sister had been brought low near Thanksgiving by a stroke that would revisit her twice in the next month. Advent, thus altered, was not anticipation. It was worry. And it seemed never to end, not even well beyond Christmas. My sister would spend months in the hospital, many weeks in intensive care.

Rather than the glories of Isaiah, we faced sorrow. Not blooming, but fading; not splendor, but weakness; not strength, but feebleness; not firmness, but frailty. Eyes saw less;

ears heard less. There was no leaping. Singing was difficult; joy and gladness, rare.

It was one family's way of suffering hardship—not the dramatic and terrible losses that so many millions feel, but a searing pain nonetheless. We were blessed by family and friends, attended by medicine with its high technology and personal care, but we fought anguish.

The words of St. James seemed a cool rebuke, if not a cruel joke. "Be patient. See how the farmer awaits the precious yield of the soil. He looks forward to it patiently while the soil receives the winter and spring rains. You, too, must be patient. Steady your hearts, because the coming of the Lord is at hand."

Yet patience just did not work. My sister was the soul of patience—she had abundant gratitude for the slightest things—but each day seemed to get worse. Hospital windows seemed to sprout bars. Intensive care was a sentence without parole, without promise of deliverance.

When John the Baptist was in prison, he heard about the things Jesus was doing; so he sent his disciples to inquire: "Are you 'he who is to come,' or do we look for another?" Jesus said to tell John "what you hear and see: The blind recover their sight, cripples walk, lepers are cured, the deaf hear, dead are raised to life and the poor have the good news preached to them." But this particular cripple did not walk; she did not even get up. Every attempt brought a setback.

Still, Advent makes promises. God will hear the cry of the poor. The small, the broken, the weak, the needy will have their time to rejoice.

The first changes came in us—we, the solicitous but power-less. Seeing my sister in her weakness and suffering unblocked some new pulse in us. Never was it so clear to our family how much our hearts went out to her. Surely we care about parents, brothers, sisters, and children, but it is often only in their poverty that we realize how much we love them. Two brothers agreed one day that they had never fully known how much they loved and admired their sister. Thus they experienced the ways that, even in our poverty (perhaps especially then), a love that can only be called godly is born. We, the image of God who made us, are touched by the poor beloved.

In some way, Advent never let go of us last year. True, in the spring we would later celebrate the Christmas we had missed. But the hold of Advent remained. This is a truth I will not forget. It is a truth that all of us on this earth must acknowledge, whether we are numbered among the "poor of the world," or whether our poverty is revealed only in our illness, our aging, or our dying.

We humans will always be in Advent. A year's Christmas may come, regeneration may occur, but at the core of our being is an endless waiting. We are utterly indigent when measured by eternity. "Come, Lord Jesus" is a song not only for December. It is a refrain for our entire lives, all our days.

For the world and all its life is only Advent. It is a creation unfinished, a groaning for another wondrous coming, a second birth. Our final happiness and healing, rich or poor, will not be quarried here. We who believe that heaven once came down to earth also believe that every grace of the earth will be lifted to undying life by our God made flesh.

And for my sister, who revealed the deeper mystery of Advent to me, she is given yet another Christmas on earth. This and every following Christmas will occasion fresh gratitude. Although she had seemed so caught in winter, the spring did come. There has been healing, and in her healing we saw a courage and strength previously untapped. The prolonged process of recovery and regeneration gave birth to new depth and resilience in her. Things unseen before were now recognized and named. Words previously unsaid and unheard were given utterance. The voiceless spoke. Stricken, she walked again.

Even if the healing had not been launched by the turn of spring, even if Advent had never really ended for us, a new incarnation had taken place. We had found more good to love than expected. We had seen more truth to know than once imagined. And the word of love had again been made flesh, having germinated in the somber days of a long winter.

4. Joseph

Is. 7:10–14; Rom. 1:1–7; Mt. 1:18–24

"He received her into his home as his wife."

Was it good news for Joseph when the angel appeared and told him about Isaiah's "virgin with child"? Was he thrilled that Mary would give birth to a baby boy called Immanuel? The angel was speaking, we may presume, of the woman Joseph loved. "Have no fear about taking Mary as your wife. It is by the Holy Spirit that she has conceived this child."

This was supposed to be a consoling message, given as it was by an angel. But I've wondered now and then whether Joseph ever had any negative thoughts about the whole thing. Is it possible that he experienced a tiny twinge of jealousy about the Holy Spirit? This may seem preposterous to say, but at times Joseph may have wondered whether it was a dream he had or a nightmare.

I've often thought about the incident in somewhat literal, realistic terms. Here is this man betrothed to a woman who is going to bear a child that is not his own "flesh and blood." Everything is already worked out: the child will be a boy and have the name of Jesus. It's one thing to believe that such an event could occur. It is quite another to accept it and take joy in it. I wonder if Joseph ever felt he was in some way robbed. Anyway, when Joseph awoke, he did as the angel directed and welcomed Mary into his home.

Even if we assume that Joseph was happy with the prospect

of being a foster father to this future savior of his people, things did not work out very well. In fact, just about everything was botched up. Instead of security and comfort, they found themselves facing a treacherous journey during the last stage of Mary's pregnancy. So much for well-wrought plans that any father, foster or not, would want to make. They would have no suitable place to stay, no family or friends around. The earliest days would be full of fear and flight. The first ceremony in the temple would be marred by the ominous prediction of an old seer that his son would be rejected and his wife would have her very soul pierced.

After the early years of migration and displacement, even when the family finally settled down, there was more trouble. The lad would be misplaced in Jerusalem and, after a three-day search, he would show up reminding them that he had another "Father" who made a greater claim on him.

Joseph, the foster father of Jesus, was the man who would be Christians' historic image of the good provider, the protector. Did he feel like that, this man of flesh and blood, this decent and just man? Was it a struggle for him to believe that any good would come of it?

Whatever he may have felt, as an earthly father he must have died a thousand deaths caring for that woman and child, both of whom he had accepted in faith as belonging finally to One other than himself. So it is with every true parent, every true spouse.

He became our patron of a happy death. This probably happened because he was thought to have died in their presence. It may also be because by then he was such a free and open man.

5. Subversive Celebration

Is. 9:1–6; Tit. 2:11–14; Lk. 2:1–14

"A joy to be shared."

Although I've never read the tale or seen the film, reliable sources tell me that "How the Grinch Stole Christmas" is about a jealous critter, posing as Santa Claus, who steals all the gifts set aside for children. A little girl spies the theft; the rest of the children, undaunted by their loss, celebrate Christmas anyway.

There are all sorts of Grinches who steal Christmas. Just think of the moves to call it "Xmas" or of Christmas stamps without the Madonna and Child. Less overtly, we are treated to phrases like "Happy Holidays" and "Season's Greetings." In a way, that's robbery. After all, the only reason we are celebrating is a baby whose birth changed the course of history. Even some theologians seem to steal Christmas away with pronouncements that such a miracle could never have happened.

Like the young girl and all her friends in the story, the little ones—the little people—somehow celebrate Christmas anyway.

Perhaps that's how Christmas celebrations actually got started in the early fourth century. If the Roman emperor insisted on having his birthday celebrated, the little people decided that they would celebrate the birth of Jesus. If the cultural powers worshiped the sun god at the year's end, Christians would exalt the Son of God.

The high and mighty eventually caught on. By the year 500, the church made Christmas a special feast. Three decades later, the Roman Empire followed suit. Commemorating the birth of Jesus spread throughout Europe; and by 600, Augustine of Canterbury baptized ten thousand converts on that holy day. For almost a millennium, Christmas was the special feast of the poor, the common people, the little ones.

By the sixteenth century, however, with its political, national, and ecclesiastical wars, Christmas was disappearing from many places. The Puritans condemned and abolished Christmas as something pagan and idolatrous. They even tried to make observing it a sin. In 1642 services were banned. No decorations were allowed. Two years later Christmas was declared a time of fast and penance. In 1647 Parliament, that corporate Grinch, totally banned Christmas. Markets were ordered to stay open. Longer work hours were enforced. The little people did not like this at all. There were riots. Ten thousand people demonstrated in Kent.

The monarchy, thinking that plum pudding, mince pie, goose, and "good will" could make up for the theft, allowed for secular celebration, not wanting to seem a Scrooge. But even in the 1700s, when Charles Wesley was penning "Hark, the Herald Angels Sing," a more refined mind pronounced: "There is no place for Christmas in the modern world."

Although Christmas was outlawed in New England until 1850, and people were forced to work that day while their children were ordered to school, subversive practices from olden times persisted. Folklore defied the Grinches: there were reports of cattle and deer on their knees, birds singing in the snow, bees humming in harmony, animals talking. Trees, decked with fruit, promised a new Eden. Breaded wafers and glowing candles hung from branches.

As it was then, so it will be. There is a mystery in Christmas far brighter than presents, more persistent than the great wars or personal sorrows that seem to steal it away. Christmas is about the child who became the bread of life, the baby who beamed as the light of the world.

The Grinch, by the way, had a change of heart. Apparently what did the trick was seeing the joy of children.

6. Holy Ground

Num. 6:22–27; Gal. 4:4–7; Lk. 2:16–21

"Pondered in the heart."

A tendency found in many religions is to escape, sometimes even negate, the ordinary. The Buddha finds enlightenment after leaving home, friends, attachments. The yoga path of Hinduism is an ascending detachment from family, business, relationships. The Greek ideal of truth is the world of forms, while the life of time and senses is illusion. Christianity itself has had its traditions of flight—from marriage, the city, the "world," even if it meant being a hermit sitting on a pole above and beyond everyone else.

But the heart of Christianity is a transformation of the ordinary, not a flight from it. After all, Incarnation, the central mystery we embrace, affirms that the eternal Word *becomes* flesh, not flees it.

We are, in this respect, children of Judaism, whose God of Moses and the prophets enters space and time, deeply concerned about and profoundly moved by our condition. The most ancient covenant of Abraham arises from his relationship to Sarah—her childlessness, her laughter, the baby she finally nursed in old age. Abraham's mighty faith was tested in relationship to his son—his prize possession, his guarantee of immortality.

In the Christmas narratives, ordinary people like shepherds and travelers are the messengers of God, not just angels, and certainly not the power-brokers of nations.

Zechariah in his doubts and dumbness, Elizabeth finding God in her cousin, Joseph coping with the demands of Caesar—taxes, housing, and relocation—all encounter God. A simple, devout old man like Simeon still searches, still hopes, and finally sees. Another old prophet, Anna, still praying in the temple sixty years after her husband's death—when one might think there was not much more to look forward to—discovers the truth.

And then this holy family, these people. Cousins and aunts and acquaintances. A mother who is mother of one child, yet mother of us all. Her spouse, a man, a worker, a father of a child somehow not fully his. They are ordinary people who find the place where strength and wisdom and favor might flourish.

It is first and foremost in our relationships, our families, our friends, that God is encountered, that faith is given flesh, that our theories of justice are tested out, that our prayer is made real, that dreams are actualized.

Even the great mystic teacher St. Teresa of Avila insisted on that truth: when people came inquiring about the heights of holy prayer, she would ask how their relationships were going. And the great skeptic Freud knew it, too: the stage of the ordinary, of the family, was where the deepest dramas were played out.

Our most profound sufferings, our greatest heroics, our most significant encounters with God are here with these people we know and love, in their goodness, in their weakness. Where else do we most intimately encounter what Paul calls the "requirements" of love: those crucibles of patience, the winnowing of humility, the courage of forgiveness, the comfort of kindness.

It is one rather easy thing to love humanity. It is quite another to love this one, who is so close to me, so like me.

But when it happens, there is glory, even if the sword pierces the heart.

A man entrusts his only son, merely twenty-eight but at the gate of death, to the arms of God.

A woman sees every one of her brothers and sisters die—and she trusts.

A young son goes to his parents with news that is first sad, and then is transformed, like a butterfly, into soaring grace.

A spouse forgives the great wound of infidelity.

A child gives the mother a flower, so unexpected, for the first time.

A husband cares for a wife, who has multiple sclerosis, for twenty years. After she parts from this world, he himself, suddenly unmoored in the abyss of Alzheimer's, is cared for by the daughter he once had to forgive.

A mother still stands by and with her teenager who seems neither kind nor appreciative.

It is all here, in our homes, in the pews of our churches, in our friends, in our families.

Here is the holy ground. Here is the face of God, the smile shining upon us, the kindly gaze upon us. These are arks of the covenant. These are the holy of holies if we only look, like Simeon; if we only see, like Anna; if only, like Mary, we take time to ponder it all in our hearts.

7. Defending the Child

Is. 60:1–6; Eph. 3:2–6; Mt. 2:1–12

"Rachel weeping for her children."

The feast of Epiphany has the makings of high drama. It features long journeys, guiding stars, ominous danger, holy dreams, great escapes, and a threatened baby.

Epiphany's conflicts are boldly drawn. Light fights night. The joy of discovery ends long wandering. Truth foils deception.

The Magi symbolize our noblest human efforts. They are

wise ones, star-gazers, people of philosophy, science, and treasure.

They go trekking for the truth. Finding it, they give
homage, not to the high and mighty Herod, but to the child of
the Most High.

Herod is not only a liar and a killer, he is afraid. He is
threatened by the child, this defenseless babe who has no
power other than the strength to engage our hope.

Why do the Herods of history fear the children of the
world? Could it be the fear of love? Why does the Herod in us
fear the child in us? Could it be that we are scared by hope?
Could it be that we dread the love drained from us by the
defenseless other?

In our own day, the child in our midst is at risk. The
wonder and awe of the child embarrass our utilitarian minds.
The child's vulnerability and dependency shame our inau-
thentic desires for control. And so we kill the child within.

The children outside of us are also under attack. They die of
dysentery in Baghdad, as victims of a "clean" war, an ugly
dictator, and indifferent nations. Children are the easiest of
the enemy to slaughter: little Muslims in the Balkans, tiny
Catholics in Sudan, toddling Hutu or Tutsi in Rwanda, the
unborn ripped from the wombs of Algerian women. Since they
are seen only as future soldiers, would-be enemies of the
Herodian state, it is merely a pre-emptive strike to kill them.

Children torment the occupants of a self-indulgent culture.
How could they not afflict a people bent on instant gratifica-
tion, broken promises, and narcissism? True, we can mold our
children into images of our own egos, but even that takes time
and discipline. It is easier to abandon them, to terminate
millions in our wombs, to strand the unwanted child, unpar-
ented, unattended, uneducated.

In our day we witness children drowned by their mothers,
children used as vendetta (even to the extent of pulling the
child from a murdered mother's womb), children abused by
those entrusted with their care and protection. A president

cannot even bring himself to admit that the so-called "partial-birth" abortion is actually infanticide. How could we not think that children are expendable?

Herodian consciousness clings to deceit. It must repress the truth. It plots to seduce the seeker of wisdom.

The embracers of Epiphany resist. They search out the child. They exercise wisdom in humble homage. They dream of another way.

And the dream is this: all our wisdom, our science, our gifts of human treasure, must not be pimps for the tyranny of tribe, class, nation, or ego. These oppressors survive on murderous lies. In the Epiphany dream, all our gifts will be laid at the feet of the child, not only in Bethlehem, but in all the cities of the world.

Epiphany is not only a dramatic feast. It is a missionary feast as well. Its message is for the nations. And if people of faith do not proclaim it, our children will be left to the Herods of the world.

8. Restoring the Fall

Is. 49:3–6; 1 Cor. 1:1–3; Jn. 1:29–34

"Who takes away the sin of the world."

Albert Camus wrote, I believe, the most incisive account of what our "fallen nature" would be without the Lamb of God that John the Baptist announced.

The Fall is a monologue-novel narrated by one Jean-Baptiste Clamence ruminating in an Amsterdam bar about a civilization of empty silhouettes interested only in fornication and entertainment.

Clamence is a fictional John the Baptist, "clamoring" in a

wilderness stripped of love and hope. "When all is said and done, that's really what I am ... an empty prophet for a shabby time, an Elijah without a Messiah." As opposed to John the Baptist who saw the Spirit descend like a dove to rest on Jesus, Clamence sights some doves that seem unable to find a place to land or some face to bless as beloved.

The title of the book refers to the "fall of man," that moment of succumbing to the lie, that victory of the great deceiver, the snake of seduction. But since there is no messiah to be found, seduction rules the earth, lies control our minds. "Truth," Clamence says, "is a colossal bore."

There is no God, no truth, not even the truth of a person outside of Clamence's ego who might merit his respect or win his love. Having no savior to announce, Clamence can only proclaim himself. Everything is to be used at the service of his narcissism. There are only two kinds of people he can relate to: dead ones and slaves. His whole life is devoted to denying any duty to which he might be held responsible or any morality by which he might be judged. "The essential is being able to permit oneself everything."

Camus is saying that this radical self-centeredness is the essence of sin. And if we humans cannot be healed or delivered from this moral sickness, we are condemned to an endless hate not unlike Satan's. "How intoxicating to feel like God the Father. . . . I sit enthroned among my bad angels. . . . I understand without forgiving, and above all, I feel at last that I am being adored!"

In his own life, Albert Camus apparently could not bring himself to fully believe the beloved whom John the Baptist named. But he knew that such a savior, in reversing the sin of the world and the fall of humankind, would have to be someone utterly given to the truth and wholly devoted to love.

Such a savior would not dominate men and women, but would free them. Such a savior, far from wanting slaves, would be a servant. Instead of killing for the truth, he would die for it. Instead of feeding on others, he would become their food and drink.

The true John the Baptist, unlike Camus's Jean-Baptiste Clamence, never postured as a pseudo-god. He preached not self-justification, but repentance and reform. He sought not to increase, but to decrease. And one day, as Jesus approached, he saw the Spirit-dove descend upon God's Chosen One.

Two thousand years later, Christ's followers continue to say the Baptist's words: "This is the Lamb of God, the one who has come to take away the sins of the world."

And they banquet with the bread of life.

9. Divided Hearts, Divided Church

Is. 8:23–29; 1 Cor. 1:10–13, 17; Mt. 4:12–23

"I belong to Apollos!"

By Isaiah's account, "The people who walked in darkness have seen a great light; upon those who dwelt in the land of gloom a light has shone. You have brought them abundant joy and great rejoicing." We Christians take that as a prophecy not only about Christ's coming, but also about his people.

And yet so often in the life of the church, Christ is divided into pieces, and the song of his people is cacophony. Divisions afflict the various Christian tribes. The rod of the taskmaster, which Jesus was foretold to smash, is wielded by factions who think they have cornered Christ.

In the Catholic church, it often goes like this: I am for Ratzinger. I am for Rahner. I am the Pope's. I am for protest. I'm for restoration. I'm for reform. I'm for women. I'm for tradition.

We're forgetting something: Has Ratzinger or Rahner saved

us? Is it the Pope who has been crucified for us? Have we been baptized in the name of tradition or of change?

Paul begs the Corinthians, in the name of Jesus, that there be no factions among them: "Rather be united in mind and judgment." But what unites them if they share no common ground? What unifies the formation of their judgment? It is evident that the reported "quarreling" in the church at Corinth was based upon divergent commitments to someone or something other than Jesus. That's what was splitting them apart.

The factionalist, whether of Paul's time or our own, "belongs" to someone other than Jesus. Some think that Paul has the truth. Others cling to Apollos. Others pledge their allegiance to Peter. Yet Paul will have no truck with this line of thought.

"Has Christ, then, been divided into parts? Was it Paul who was crucified for you?" Our baptism, through the gifts of tradition and law, ritual and order, is the sign of our salvation; but the salvation is found in Christ, no one, no thing else. Other voices that offer us another savior speak the worldly language of power and privilege, not the way of the cross, which to them seems inadequate and foolish.

In Matthew's Gospel Jesus leaves Nazareth for Capernaum to fulfill the promise of bringing light to the Jordan. He preached that the Kingdom of God requires reform. Indeed it does. So it was for the church of Peter and Paul. So it is for us today.

In the "always reforming" life of the church, at least two principles seem important. First, every one of us, from pope to pauper, from theologian to activist, from grandparent to child, stands humbly before God as a sinner called to conversion and salvation in Jesus Christ. There can be no other ground or principle from which we can approach our various gifts or deficiencies.

Second, it is good to recall the kinds of people Jesus chose for Apostles: from the fishermen brothers, Simon and Andrew, to Matthew and John, they were all flawed yet graced. They would go on to heal and preach a kingdom that would draw millions to Christ. And what always helped them overcome their differences was the sure knowledge that it was in Christ's name they were fishing, not their own.

10. Nietzsche's Nemesis

Zeph. 2:3, 3:12–13; 1 Cor. 1:26–31; Mt. 5:1–12

"What the world considers absurd."

Zephaniah wanted God's people to seek justice and pursue humility. But he knew that such a community would always be a minority. "I will leave as a remnant in your midst a people humble and lowly, who will take refuge in the name of the Lord."

Such are the people Jesus calls: not necessarily wise, as humans account wisdom, nor vastly influential, nor well born, but surely countercultural in the way they address the secular order. "God chose those whom the world considers absurd to shame the wise. He singled out the weak to shame the strong. He chose the low and despised, who count for nothing, to reduce to nothing those who were something; so that mankind can do no boasting before God."

It is Christ who is our justice, our redemption, our sanctification, our wisdom. This confounds any mentality which seeks self-justification or pursues fulfillment through earthly goods. To such a mind-set, Christ's wisdom is unrealistic, even foolhardy. It certainly contradicts our way of imagining human happiness.

Just look at the Sermon on the Mount to get a sense of Jesus' radical reversal of our common sense. We want abundance, control, and authority to conquer the kingdoms of the earth. His wisdom affirms that only the poor in spirit can achieve the reign of God.

We want more than all else to avoid pain and suffering. In fact most of our operating ethical systems rest upon the principle of maximizing pleasure. Yet Jesus says that those who open themselves to sorrow will find ultimate consolation.

We bristle at being overlooked, passed by, neglected, unappreciated. "We're number one" is the roaring chant of our arenas, our nationalism, our special-interest groups, our petty hurts. But Jesus says that the lowly inherit the land.

We scavenge to inflate ourselves with things, projects, people; but the Sermon on the Mount counsels us to abide in our hunger for holiness, to live with a thirst for justice.

With divided hearts and tawdry desires, we wonder why we still feel so unhappy. He says that in purity of heart and wholeheartedness we find bliss and see God.

And peacemakers? Those do-gooders, those bleeding hearts? See how far that will get them in this "real" world. Most often they are held in contempt, even by Christians.

Perhaps that is why Jesus thinks his followers will be persecuted for holiness' sake. His wisdom is such an insult to natural cleverness, the Sermon on the Mount will be ridiculed as "wimpdom," not wisdom.

Friedrich Nietzsche scoffed at the Beatitudes as prescriptions for sheep and slaves. He knew what a devastating challenge Christ was to his visions of the "superman." It was only fitting, then, that when old Nietzsche titled his last howl of power and aggression, he called it the Anti-Christ.

Still, Nietzsche saw the revolutionary import of Christ's teachings. It has been the fate of some Christians blithely to bear the name of Christ without ever having weighed his startling words.

11. Christian Faith and Politics

Is. 58:7–10; 1 Cor. 2:1–5; Mt. 5:13–16

"Salt of the earth."

The Sermon on the Mount is often taken as Jesus' list of private recommendations for a select few followers. And yet he is revealing the fundamental conditions of discipleship in his kingdom. He is speaking not only to his closest chosen friends, but to hearers at large. The sermon ends, mind you, with, "His teachings made a deep impression on the people because he taught them with authority, and not like their own scribes."

Much of the sermon, of course, was not new. After all, Jesus came from Isaiah's people who were commanded to share bread with the hungry, shelter the oppressed and homeless, and clothe the naked. Isaiah wanted his nation to shine like a light, breaking forth as the dawn. "If you remove from your midst oppression, false accusation and malicious speech; if you bestow your bread on the hungry and satisfy the afflicted, then light shall rise for you in the darkness."

With his announcement of the kingdom, Jesus, like Isaiah, makes clear that he is calling his followers to have an impact on their world. After the Beatitudes and just before his teachings on radical trust, money, and forgiveness, he challenges his listeners to live out their discipleship precisely in the context of their culture and world.

"You are the salt of the earth. But what if salt goes flat? How can you restore its flavor? You are the light of the world. A city set on a hill cannot be hidden. You do not light a lamp and then put it under a bushel basket. You set it on a stand where it gives light to all." Those who are enlisted in Jesus' kingdom must let the light of faith shine before the world so that praise might be given to God.

Jesus seems aware that we may be tempted to hide our faith. We might repress it in our public lives, presuming that it has nothing to offer the "real" world of politics and economics. Or we may just keep it under a basket—a "private" matter that makes no difference to society.

A second temptation is related to the first. If we think that our faith really makes no difference in the "real" world, it goes flat. It has nothing special to offer the world. Having lost its special taste, it never changes culture. It just mimics it.

In our own day, we have our own special complications. There are many people who seem to put their Christian faith on a pedestal for all to see, but it's a faith whose authentic flavor has gone flat. Imagine the irony of a Christian political movement which trumpets the priorities of public prayer, military security, tax cuts for the well-to-do, and capital punishment.

As one "born-again" former Catholic put it in *The American Enterprise* magazine, he's "pro-life, pro-free market, patriotic, pro-national defense, pro-gun, and anti-welfare state." I get the pro-life part, but the other stuff doesn't ring a bell when I think of Christ's teachings.

This is not a put-down of any particular political party, even though at first sight it may seem so. Close examination of the dominant parties in the United States today will show that both of them are in the pockets of the rich and powerful, both of them neglect the poor (although they use different rhetoric to cover their negligence), both of them are nationalistic, and both of them underwrite health, immigration, and labor policies that hurt the most vulnerable in society.

A Representative Hyde is very Christian in his defense of unborn babies, but I wonder what he thinks of capital punishment, capital gains, and military adventures. A Senator Kennedy rises as a great defender of women and the poor—but only as long as they are not snuggled in a womb somewhere or oppressed in a "most favored" trading nation. Cultural "conservatives" may talk about the moral rot of society, but how often do they link it up to capitalism and a me-first mentality?

If we are honest with ourselves, we will discover that our Christian faith functions little if at all in our political life. The talk is talked, but the walk is not walked. Lip service is paid, but almost every other kind of service is paid to our cultural dogmas. Just spend some time reading the Sermon on the Mount in the coming weeks, and ask yourself whether our Americanized Christianity is a light in dark times or salt for the earth.

Our faith, as St. Paul writes, is not communicated by the eloquence of high-sounding words or worldly wisdom. Clever argument and jaded rationalization are the very tools most often used to explain our faith away. The wisdom of a crucified God and the teachings of the Christ give little consolation and support to an acculturated mind.

Can a politician, then, give witness to evangelical faith? Can any of us? I think, yes. But it will require of us an admission of how readily we compromise the revolutionary message of Jesus. Upon that admission, we might then discover a Christian politics that illuminates the world far more brilliantly than the dim ideologies we guide our lives by.

12. The Revolution Jesus Announced

Sir. 15:15–20; 1 Cor. 2:6–10; Mt. 5:17–37

"Not a wisdom of this age."

The wisdom of Sirach places a radical choice before us. It is a choice between life and death, and our chosen option will be given to us. God, mighty in power and penetrating in vision, knows our hearts and our minds. Our desires and our thoughts, however, deviate from God's will.

When Paul writes to the Corinthians, he is well aware that their sophistication is no match for "the deep things of God." He urges, rather, the wisdom of the spiritually mature. But it is surely not the wisdom of this age, "nor of the rulers of this age." Such so-called wisdom can only lead to destruction. To Paul, the revelation of Jesus represents a vision that human eyes have never seen, a voice that human ears have never heard. It is beyond our wildest imaginings, "Nor has it so much as dawned on man what God has prepared for those who love him."

Indeed, it is hard to imagine any merely human prudence or wisdom conjuring up the radical propositions of the Sermon on the Mount. While Jesus does not intend to abolish the Old Law, he promises to fulfill or realize the law in a new way. And it is new, utterly at odds with the secular and religious rulers of his time. "I tell you, unless your holiness surpasses that of the scribes and Pharisees you shall not enter the kingdom of God."

Murder had already been forbidden in the Ten Commandments, but Jesus plumbs to the heart of murderous intent. It is unspoken anger, violent language, quiet contempt of the other. It is an unwillingness to forgive. "If you bring your gift to the altar and there recall that your brother has anything against you, leave your gift at the altar, go first to be reconciled with your brother, and then come and offer your gift."

How different would our own Eucharists be if we took Jesus seriously? The resentments we hold against our parents, our children, our spouses, and our neighbors would have to dissolve before we would approach the altar, lest we receive the sacrament unworthily. Perhaps that is why our Communion is aptly prefaced by the sign of peace. Just as we ask God, "Look not on our sins, but on the faith of your church," so also we who have sinned against each other must see with the eyes of faith and forgive.

Adultery was forbidden of old. But Jesus speaks to the lust that underlies the adultery. (Remember how Jimmy Carter was ridiculed when he admitted to lust in his heart? He was just admitting what we all know but are ashamed to acknowledge.)

Jesus unmasks the injustice (especially against women) and the adultery that so often accompany divorce. His words are strong, but no stronger than those addressed to us who refuse to forgive.

In matters of discipleship Jesus does not allow ifs, ands, or buts. "Say 'Yes' when you mean 'Yes' and 'No' when you mean 'No.' Anything beyond that is from the evil one."

It can be dangerous, mind-altering, to read the Sermon on the Mount. It will shake the ways we think about punishment, penalty, justice, and love itself. Most of all it thwarts our attempts to compromise our faith or set aside privileged parts of our lives that we shield from the law of God.

"If your right eye is your trouble, gouge it out and throw it away. . . . If your right hand is your trouble, cut it off and throw it away. Better to lose part of your body than to have it all cast into Gehenna."

What can we make of all this? The Lord's teachings seem futile. Our meager hearts feel diminished by his standards. Who of us has not broken promises, or harbored resentment, or acted lustfully, or sworn vengeance, or faked our way through the day?

In one of his earliest retreat talks, the late Anthony DeMello, S.J., said as much. We all fall short. And therefore we all must not judge. We all are called to holiness, and therefore we must not exempt ourselves.

The Sermon on the Mount is not there to cast us down into helpless and hopeless guilt. No, it is an invitation to that high holiness that we have hitherto not seen or heard about. It is an excavation into our deepest loves, so that seeing what we love most, we will finally be given our heart's desire. But it is a harrowing trip down into the mines of our motivation.

Journeying through the gospels is no easy trip. It's a dangerous, plummeting, careening journey. Anyone who talks, writes, or preaches about the gospel in a way that leaves us unchallenged or bored just isn't doing the work. Any teenager who leaves church without having witnessed the radicalness of the Mass and the revolutionary import of the gospel was either asleep or listening to a sleeping minister of the Eucharist.

We may think our faith is just another "amen" to the wisdom of our age. Well, if we think that, we just don't know what our faith is about.

13. Militant Faith

Lev. 19:1–2, 17–18; 1 Cor. 3:16–23; Mt. 5:38–48

"Love your enemies."

The Sermon on the Mount is so baffling, we either have to ignore it or pretend we never heard it. Those tactics failing, we turn it inside out. The first time I came across such a strategy was after a lecture I gave on "Capital Punishment and Disarmament in the Light of the Gospels." My assigned task was apparently not very successfully accomplished. From the back of the room came a courageous dissenting voice. "How can you be against war and capital punishment? Even Christ said, 'an eye for an eye, a tooth for a tooth.'"

What can one do? Why even say that the very next sentence of Jesus in Matthew continues: "But what I say to you is: offer no resistance to injury. When a person strikes you on the right cheek, turn and offer him the other"?

We've had these words since the beginning of our church, and by and large we still act as if Jesus said, "an eye for an eye." Even if we finally acknowledge that Jesus did solemnly tell us to turn the other cheek, in our more candid moments we admit that we think it's outrageous.

Sometimes I feel everything in my being recoils from the

words of Jesus. I want even more than an eye for an eye. And who has a right to ask me for an extra shirt, much less a coat? I reluctantly give up a minute of service, much less a mile. Go two miles? Love enemies? It's hard enough to love those close at hand.

When I see my own resistance to the gospels, how can I be surprised that our church seems to ignore what he said? How can I be upset if a nation would think it sheer idiocy? Try forgiving the creep down the street, much less Saddam Hussein.

Our resistance to the gospel is all of a piece. To hold myself not accountable is to hold my nation or church not accountable. To exempt my nation or church from the truth is to exempt myself.

In *The Old Testament without Illusion,* biblical scholar John L. McKenzie notes that Christians have felt compelled to create and honor a political ethic where Christ is useless. But such a maneuver invites tragedy, because the political is always in some way personal, and the personal, political. When we make decisions as a nation or a church as if the Incarnation has not happened and Jesus has not died, personal imitation sooner or later follows suit.

The way of Jesus stands in contrast to our personal wars as well as our public ones. As McKenzie puts it, "You cannot be a Christian in private and a secularist every place where your life impinges upon the public; or, to steal another phrase, you cannot serve God and Mammon." McKenzie goes on to say that Christians who think they can serve both God and Mammon support just wars. The same can be said for capital punishment.

It is not easy. The demons of the world and of our hearts seduce us into thinking that the ways of God cannot be followed in this time-bound journey. Even the commands that the Lord gave to Moses seemed so impractical. "Speak to the whole Israelite community and tell them: Be holy, for I, the Lord your God, am holy." They were to have no hatred for brother or sister, to take no revenge, to cherish no grudge against fellow citizens, to love their neighbors as themselves. So the Israelites, like all nations, all peoples, weighed the shrewdness of the world, of self-defense, of retaliation, on a balance with the wisdom of God.

For myself, what got me to speak less confidently about capital punishment and forgiveness of enemies was the terrible murder of a young girl, the daughter of a friend of mine. He was a fellow professor at the university and a deacon in a local parish. I found myself avoiding him, especially after the murderers were caught and put on trial. I knew full well that he was aware of my facile arguments against capital punishment, and I was almost ashamed to have him look at me.

Finally one day we were suddenly on the same elevator; I could not escape. I murmured how difficult it must be to go through the trial, reliving his great loss once again. "Yes," he said, "but the hardest thing is trying to convince the prosecutors that we want life imprisonment without parole and not the death penalty. He doesn't understand that we follow Christ in all of this."

Here was someone, profoundly injured by an unjust aggressor, who really believed and wanted to practice the words of Jesus. He really believed in a God who gives sun and rain to the unjust as well as the just. He really aspired to a love made perfect in the Crucified who asked forgiveness for enemies. He had entered the mystery of which Paul spoke. He knew that all things were his, and he was Christ's, and Christ was God's.

"Are you not aware that you are the temple of God and that the Spirit of God dwells in you: If anyone destroys God's temple, God will destroy him. For the temple of God is holy, and you are that temple." So also, somehow, is the criminal and the enemy, despite the empty wisdom of the worldly wise.

14. Unmasking the Great Deception

Gen. 2:7–9, 3:1–7; Rom. 5:12–19; Mt. 4:1–11

"The gift is not like the offense."

A wise old spiritual director in the British Isles is reported to have said, "There is a little bit of the fake in all of us."

If he was correct, his insight may have had something to do with original sin. The Eden story was, remember, a drama woven of pretense and cover-up. Adam and Eve were the first to bite on a big lie: the denial of our creaturely dependence.

We do seem to master the art of denial at an early age. Witness the clever words of the "innocent" toddler accusing someone on the other side of the room as the milk is spilled, "See what you made me do?" Soon after infancy, we invent playmates to blame for our own blunders. "Jimmy did it." As teenagers we imagine some pretense, some "aura," which will make up for the terrible inadequacy we feel. A few put on the pose of the outsider, some play it hot, others stay cool. The cover of designer clothes helps, as an advertisement for Nike burbles, "Good clothes won't laugh at us behind our backs." Even facing marriage, some are hounded by the fear that a future spouse might find out what they are really like and then reject them.

We so much want to look good, to seem more intelligent or composed or virtuous than we are. We don roles: "Father Joe Relevant," "Sister Mary Renewal," "the perfect couple," "the success story," "the saint," "the picture of health."

"Looking good is everything," a chorus of consumer hucksters screams. Even the postmodern halls of academe have announced the inescapable fact that everything we do is a masquerade for strategies of privilege and pleasure. Pretense marks the "real world" of school corridors, unfriendly streets, and political platforms. Cover-ups not only bring down presidencies, they haunt everyday life. As Freud said, the major barrier to healing is the wounded person who asks for help but is secretly unwilling to face the truth that healing requires.

Is deception something we have to learn? Is it bred in the bones? Is it the fatal flaw of every human?

Adam and Eve, we are told, had almost everything. The only drawback was the fact that they were creatures of limit. They were good, but not God. They could have the fruit of every tree except the tree of limits, the tree of creatureliness.

It was their creaturehood that made them susceptible to the Lie.

Enter the serpent, that cunning beast, that lord of lies, who taunted their obedience and reliance on God. "Not any of the trees?" (No, they could have all the trees but one.) "Do you not want to live forever?" (But they already could eat of the tree of life.)

Ah, but the attraction of having no limits. To be God. To be self-sufficient, self-made. The pretense was attractive, desirable. The ruse looked so wise.

Thus sin entered the world, St. Paul writes, through one act: the lie of self-sufficiency. That was the offense. And it would be righted by one act as well: a life of utter truth. That was the gift.

The temptations the devil fed to Jesus were nothing other than delusions we all dream of in our longing for radical independence.

"Become your own food." Be self-sufficient. Display your power. But Jesus refuses. God alone will be his food.

"Show your stuff; muster your magic." Leap from the temple in full self-assurance. But Jesus will live by the word and power of God alone.

"Look out from the highest mountain and all will be given

you, if you only give yourself to the Lie." But Jesus declines the self-adoration, reserving glory for the Lord our God alone.

The sin of the first humans was to reject the condition of humanness: splendid creatures, yet nonetheless dependent on God.

The gift of the new Adam was a total acceptance of humanness, an entering so deeply into our limits, and even into the effects of our sin, that there would be no other reality to his consciousness than abandonment to the will of the one who sent him.

So what's left for us, we who are neither God nor savior? Well, to receive the truth is a great and difficult thing. That is why true confession is such a marvelous sacrament (and so rare). If we just acknowledge the simple truth of our limits and our sins before God and Christ's people, we reverse the offense of Eden and enter the gift of Calvary.

In acknowledging the lies of our own egotisms, of the great injustices of the world, of the excesses in appetite, of the woundings in relationship, of all the mean divisions in the church, we drop once again the heavy mask of deception. It falls from our faces, revealing our need.

We are sinners, dear friends. If we do not know that, we suffer a poverty of self-knowledge. But if we yield to the truth, not only that we are creatures, but that we are in sore need of redemption, we are newly free, open to love.

We reverse the big lie of Eden as we embrace the big truth of Gethsemane, now able to say with the one who graced our fallen state, "Into your hands I commend my spirit."

15. The Long Haul

Gen. 12:1–4; 2 Tim. 1:8–10; Mt. 17:1–9

"Go forth . . . I will show you."

God had called us: so says St. Paul in his Second Letter to Timothy. And Jesus is the call. Hence the voice from the clouds on the mount of transfiguration says, "Listen to him."

But what are we called to? What happens if we listen to Jesus? Most of us have been listening for years. Supposedly that is one of the reasons we still show up in church. It's his call we are heeding. He is our new Moses, our lawgiver. He is our greatest prophet, more glorious for us even than old Elijah. We've been listening to him. Now what?

So it is that we want to get on with it, to have things finished once and for all. Let there be a conversion, complete and dramatic. At least let there be some progress. We get tired of waiting. We've heard the call over and over, but not much seems to get done.

We can understand why Peter, James, and John wanted to build a tent. At least they've had a mountain experience. They saw Jesus in his glory standing with the mightiest prophet and the greatest lawgiver. No wonder they wanted to stop things right there. Surely it would be all downhill after the mountaintop. Surely there was not much more glory to see and savor.

Those of us who don't have a mountain experience tend to settle down, too. If you're fifty-five, as I am, you might well expect that there are not many more journeys to take or conversions to make. What was going to happen has pretty much happened. Even some of us who are only thirty or forty might be inclined to believe that we have finally "arrived" at the person we were becoming.

Abraham was seventy-five. At seventy-five you've pretty well seen the landscape. Not much more is to be expected.

But for Abraham it was the beginning. There was yet another call: "Go forth from the land of your kinsfolk, go away from your parents' house. I will show you. You'll know the place when you get there. I'll make a great nation of you out of nothing." Fat chance. A great nation? Blessings and high achievement unexpected? Get real.

Yet this great old man stirred to the voice of God. He gathered his family and things and hit the road. He was seventy-five.

The Jews (and we their cousins) have such great heroes. When Abraham heard a new call in his eighth decade, it was before the great famine and the tragedy of Lot and his wife, before he shared the bread and wine of Melchizedek, before he ever reached Egypt or Canaan, before the birth of Hagar's Ishmael, before he would plead on behalf of Sodom and Gomorrah.

It would take twenty-five years more for the promised covenant even to take shape, when he would be one hundred and his wife would change her name. This was all before Isaac, his prize child, long before Sarah's death and his second marriage to Keturah. It was, in fact, one hundred years before he would die. It's a good thing he hadn't settled down permanently in his seventies.

Abraham and Sarah, our parents in faith, remind us that it is not so much a matter of when this life's journey ends, as it is a matter of where the great hike of hope takes us.

When I was thirty-five, I foolishly imagined that I had seen it all. Thinking it was a sign of spiritual freedom and openness to God's will, I even told my spiritual director in India that I was willing and ready to die. "Don't say that," he said. "You can never say you've had enough."

Right he was. By the time I was forty-five, I realized that I had not dreamed, ten years earlier, of the pains that humans could suffer, the joys we might endure, the sheer exultation in life that is available to us. There is always more. There is always a further call as long as we tread this earthly road.

A woman who thinks she has had enough of her professional work discovers a new marvelous power to love and heal.

A priest at sixty-five taps into vast depths of courage and possibility within himself he had never imagined.

A man at sixty, dreaming of something new, starts a food distribution program in a poor Central American country.

A sister at fifty founds a new order.

A ninety-two-year-old nun goes more deeply into love, forgiveness, and trust than any novice could dare explore.

A couple married fifty years thanks Marriage Encounter for helping them finally understand each other.

Just think how many centuries it will take for us to delve into the mystery of God.

And so, it's true, I wouldn't resist or resent the going. We believe, after all, in the resurrection of a body far more glorious than our present meager skins. But I no longer think of rushing it. We need not build the tent here and now.

Abraham knew as much. He is our father in faith. Thank God Sarah had the faith as well.

16. Water and Bread

Ex. 17:3–7; Rom. 5:1–2, 5–8; Jn. 4:5–42

"In their thirst, they grumbled."

Jesus' encounter with the woman at the well could serve as a metaphor for our great thirst. We languish for the living water. It satisfies and refreshes. It revives and cleanses. We die without it. This is our condition: we thirst.

Existential thirst launches all our efforts. The thirst for fullness is behind every move we make, even those, St. Thomas Aquinas reminds us, that are born of our misdirected and misguided longings.

It was a mighty thirst that led Israel out of Egypt, just as it was their thirst that led them to complain that even Egypt would be better than the dry, godforsaken desert. And it was their thirst that God would slake, even from a rock. God would be their well of life just as surely as the manna-bread would fall from heaven.

Thirst led the Samaritan woman not only to a well, but to Jesus who would refresh her spirit and renew her world. It was the same thirst that drew her through all the detours, all the lovers of her life. If she could only realize, Jesus said, that he himself was the living water, the fulfillment of every hope.

At the well, Jesus was the unexpected visitor who would welcome her. He was the alien who became most intimate. He was the most strange who drew most near. He was the unknown who would know her most deeply.

St. Augustine wrote that the very one who asks for a drink promises a drink. The very one who seems to be in need, hoping to receive, is the one who is rich, wanting to give, wanting to satisfy our deepest thirsts. "Whoever drinks the water I give will never be thirsty. No, the water I give shall become a fountain within, leaping up to provide eternal life."

Receiving his truth, the woman's thirst was quenched. Believing him, yielding to his word, her desires were finally met.

In our relationship to the Christ of God, it is not only a matter of drink; it is a matter of food as well. It is manna. "Doing the will of the one who sent me and bringing that work to fullest completion is my food."

Our endless thirst is what makes us work so hard at physical life: producing, earning, consuming. Thirst, too, excites our spiritual longings, our proving and testing, our fretful striving for virtue, even for perfection. But our thirst is so great we can get lost in it and ignore the very truth that could satisfy.

That great truth is God's thirst for us, even in our sin. Remember, it is Jesus who asked the confused and searching woman for a drink. It is he who reached out to her.

When we see the full mystery of Lent and Easter, we realize that, as great as our dry thirst and wide yearning may be, it is God's eternal thirst for us, for our faith, our trust, our love, that is the central mystery of being.

Jesus is the stream of love between God and ourselves. We are invited to drink of the mystery, this outpouring of love, embodied in Jesus, the thirst of God in us. His "I thirst" from the cross is as much the voice of God as it is the stirring of a human heart. It is not Christ's humanity alone that feels the parching. It is his divinity too.

The story of the woman at the well, like our own rituals of baptism and the Eucharist, interprets for us the fundamental nature of our relationship to God. We are nothing without God. God is our drink. God is our sustenance.

There are days when we realize the deep meaning of our Eucharist, when we fully enter the actions we do and the words we say. It amounts to this: "I take you for my food and drink, my nutriment. You become my very being as food and drink become my own flesh." So great is the expanse of our hunger and thirst that only God can fill us, fulfill us.

Thus our desire is insatiable. But that is not even half the story. More vast than the furthest reach of our hunger and thirst to be known and loved is the God, eternal love and truth, who longs to be our bread of life, our living water, the sustenance that has loved us into being and keeps us there.

In the Letter to the Romans St. Paul recalls the awesome disproportion between our own aspirations and the beneficence of God. We are not to be fixated on how deep and undying our desires are, but on the vastness of God's desire for us. "At the appointed time, when we were still powerless, Christ died for us godless creatures. It is rare that anyone should lay down one's life for a just person, though it is barely possible for someone good to have such courage. It is precisely in this that God proves his love for us: that while we were still sinners, Christ died for us."

As acute and overwhelming as our thirst for God might be, as exhausting and enervating as our journeys to God might seem, the yearning that God has for us and the journey that God has made into our hearts surpass it all infinitely.

Drink it in.

17. Escape from Plato's Cave

1 Sam. 16:1, 6–7, 10–13; Eph. 5:8–14; Jn. 9:1–41

"I am the light of the world: anyone who follows me will not be walking in the dark, but will have the light of life."

Throughout the Fourth Gospel we find a range of statements in which Jesus makes solemn pronouncements about his identity and mission. They are the great "I am" sayings, which are not found in Matthew, Mark, or Luke. In the eighth chapter of John, for example, Jesus reveals that "I am he" from above, who does what the Father wishes. More startling he says, "Before Abraham was, I am"—an echo of the words uttered by the God of Moses. This transcendent implication of the "I am" is further complemented by what can only be called a litany of salvation names.

The Jesus of the Fourth Gospel portrays himself as the vine without which we would be groundless and barren. He is also the bread of life. He is the good shepherd. He is the gate. He is the way, the truth, and the life.

But what is particularly interesting in the context of the gospel story of the "man born blind" is Jesus' announcement, "I am the light of the world," which is found in both the eighth and ninth chapters.

The healed man was in physical darkness from birth. The sight Jesus gave him not only allowed him to see the world, but to embrace his healer in faith. More damaging than the man's organic lack of vision was the spiritual blindness of his neighbors and the Pharisees. They had eyes but could not see the truth. Some of them could not even accept that the cure was real, even though the man said, "I'm the one all right."

The Pharisees first reject the grace of healing under the pretext that it was done on the Sabbath. Surely good cannot come from that. Then they entertain the possibility that the poor fellow was never really blind. Even the testimony of the parents cannot convince them. The Pharisees insist that the man deny the very gift of the sight he has been given and renounce the giver. But since he assures them that Christ must be from God, they expel him from their premises. "You are steeped in sin from your birth, and you are giving us lectures?"

When Jesus seeks out the man and receives his profession of faith, he utters the paradox that the sightless see and those who think they see are really in the darkness of sin.

The Fourth Gospel's stark contrast of appearances and reality, true and erroneous opinion, light and darkness, is often seen as a result of Greek and Gnostic influences. But such contrasts are not limited to this Gospel, nor are they a theme of the Greeks alone.

We know that in the selection of David as king, the Lord told Samuel not to judge by mere appearances or by any other human standard, for God sees differently than mere humans. Paul calls his Ephesians children of a "light" that produces every kind of goodness, justice, and truth. Christ himself embodies the promise of the psalm: "The Lord is my light and my salvation; whom shall I fear?"

The story of the blind man does, however, ring a bell for anyone who has ever read "The Myth of the Cave" in Plato's *Republic*. There we find a story of all humanity chained in a darkened cave throughout life. These captives can see nothing but flickering images on a wall—shadows, appearances, illusions—which they take for reality. One prisoner, liberated from the chains, makes the arduous crawl upward to the world of the shining sun. When he returns to the cave with his tales of the new-found source of light and the life and warmth it gives, the prisoners think him crazy. They simply deny his experience. It just can't be. The chains and the amusing images on the wall are reality. Thus his conversion is ridiculed; his invitation is resisted.

This is how the Greek Plato describes the intellectual assent of the soul to truth. To contemplate divine life is to find freedom; but it is also to encounter opposition from "the evil state of man, misbehaving in a ridiculous manner, arguing over shadows and images."

Clearly there are parallels between the Platonic myth of the cave and the story of the man born blind. Each figure is given new sight. Each is rejected by the inhabitants of the old world. And even the so-called wise authorities would rather cling to their chains and discuss the shadows than embark on the journey of faith.

As opposed to Plato, however, for whom the sun was the absolute form of good, the light the blind man of the gospels saw revealed not merely an unchanging and perfect world of ideas, but the face of the Son of God. In the light of his life, those who have embraced the vision have encountered the ultimate reality: not pure being or absolute form, but an eternal community of persons in relationship. The "I am" indeed gives light and life. Far more wonderfully, our God gives and receives love.

The words of the old hymn "Amazing Grace" remind all of us who know that, once blind, we now see:

> When we've been there ten thousand years,
> Bright shining as the sun,
> We've no less days to sing God's praise
> Than when we first begun.

18. Release from the Tombs

Ez. 37:12–14; Rom. 8:8–11; Jn. 11:1–45

"I will open your graves and you will rise."

I wonder how it was when Lazarus died for the second time. Were Mary and Martha there? Most likely Jesus was not; for he, shortly after he raised Lazarus, died the death himself and, despite the Resurrection, left the sisters to grieve once again.

Of what did Lazarus eventually die? Was it a recurrence of the original affliction or something unforeseen? Did Mary and Martha, the second time around, think that Jesus could spare Lazarus anew? Martha, remember, had told Jesus, "If you had been here, my brother would not have died." Perhaps she would be bold enough to wonder out loud what the point of the earlier miracle was if Lazarus was going to die anyway.

The Fourth Gospel goes to some length to show that Lazarus was a special case, unlike the other reported miracles of restored life. First, Jesus loved Lazarus and his sisters "very much." And since his "beloved Lazarus has fallen asleep," Jesus set out (taking his dear old time) to wake him. This deliberate delay led to the second special point: Lazarus was really dead. Finished. He was wrapped up in the tomb for four days. This would not be some case of a "near-death" experience or an early version of the persistent vegetative state. Face wrapped up, bound hand and foot, Lazarus was so dead that one of his sisters warned Jesus that there would "surely be a stench."

Thus it was that another stupendous reversal took place. What was irretrievably dead would live again. What looked final was not. What seemed finished had only just begun. As Ezekiel prophesied over the valley of bones, even a people as good as dead could hope in the living God. When all was lost, much more would be found. "I will put my spirit in you that you may live. I have promised, and I will do it, says the Lord."

This promise is what I have had to rely on during these early weeks of a year when the bodies of people close to me have been consigned to tombs.

One was in her nineties, ready to go, even eager. She was apprehensive about the prospect (is the promise true? is the hope real?), but she managed to put it in Christ's hands. She had wanted to follow him and his mercy as far back as the roaring twenties—a time so strange to our own we would not recognize it. She wondered what the upshot of all those years might be, that parade of joy and sorrow, all the rotations of nations and mighty personages, all the momentous invention and art? And more: What of her life? What happened to the far-off dreams of an eighteen-year-old who knew a church that would "never" change, a liturgy that would "always" be in Latin facing the wall, a community that would always be there, thriving and growing. Has my valiant aunt really died? Is she forever in the tomb?

A second soul, forty years her junior, went suddenly, without the lingering liturgies of bedside comfort and the usual months of long-expected diminishment. No, she went too soon, before her grandmotherly days arrived, before the merited benefits of rest and refreshment. She had felt a rekindling of faith's light at the end—but so briefly seen, so quickly gone. It was extinguished. Was that once red-headed teenage girl buried eternally?

Finally a third tomb, unworthy of the loved Lazarene we brought there, the ground so impenetrably hard, its dusty surface covered with dead leaves. Surely Christ would weep at this funeral. How could he not be troubled in spirit, moved by the same deep emotion he felt at the grave of Lazarus. This young grace we grieved died in her early thirties, the age of the Jesus she emulated. Like him, she was a comet, a prophetess, a seer, and a deep, abiding, life-long friend. See how her parents and family, her husband, and her comrades so miss her. If only the Lord had been there, she might. . . . Being there, his sobs would be seen, while we would whisper under our breath, "See how much he loved her."

All death is untimely, rude, and somehow hopeless, whether of a nonagenarian or her great-grandniece, a fresh infant at death's door, bearing mortal wounds since conception. All deaths lead to dust, dry bones in valleys, dissolved bodies in tombs.

Jesus' raising of Lazarus was a holding action. So were all his other miracles. Sickness and death were just postponed. But these miracles, like the quickened, sinewed bones rising before the pie eyes of Ezekiel are also a promise. In our profession of faith, we are not asked to acquiesce in a fait accompli; we are asked to believe, to trust a promise made to us, that even though we die, we will come back to life in a love who is our resurrection. If we live and die in that belief, then with Mary, Martha, and Lazarus, with our ancient wise ones, with our veterans tested in the prime of life, and with our vivacious young whose whole being is promise, nothing of our good and grace will be lost or forgotten in tombs.

"If the Spirit of him who raised Jesus from the dead dwells in you, then the one who raised Christ from the dead will bring your mortal bodies to life also through his Spirit dwelling in you."

19. Betrayal

Mt. 21:1–11; Is. 50:4–7; Phil. 2:6–11; Mt. 26:14–27

"Jesus was to die for the nation."

Palm Sunday, now called Passion Sunday, is an uneasy union of names. Is it the day of Jesus' victorious procession into Jerusalem, recalled by our parades of palm leaves? Or is it the day of his disastrous downfall?

It is both. For the great triumphant procession of palms as well as the betrayed allegiances of the human heart are both woven into the Passion and death of Jesus.

The liturgy of Passion Sunday is a collision of themes: glorious hosannas and somber omens. Isaiah promised a servant of God who would have a "face set like flint" to brave the pummeling, spit, and ridicule. Paul's lovely hymn in Philippians is one of triumph—"every knee should bend in heaven and earth and every tongue confess"—but only after disgrace and ignominious death.

It goes unnoticed, for the most part, that the inescapable context of the Passion is a national, tribal, and political struggle. The betrayals are always hatched in the presence of looming authorities who seduce the betrayer—the Judas, the Peter, the disciple in us. You cannot avoid the sense that there is some profound geopolitical strife going on here. The stage is set for armed violence, the raised sword in the cause of right. There are secret police and public meetings of high priests, governors, assemblies. There are political prisoners. Finally, there is a crisis of authority. "Are you the king of the Jews?" Are you the king of Christians? Are you the king of Catholics?

They are questions that history poses not only to Christ, but to all who follow him. What would be our answer? Who or what is the real object of our allegiance?

In the gospel reading from the Saturday prior to every Passion/Palm Sunday, we behold the crisis of allegiance that the people of Jesus' time faced. In that gospel Jesus is condemned by a logic of self-defense and corporate survival. Chief priests and high councils are threatened by Jesus and his way. He is a menace to national and religious interests. Note the language: "If we let him go on like this, everyone will believe in him, and the Romans will come in and destroy both our holy place and our nation." Caiaphas, that "realistic" murmur of expedience in all our hearts, advises us: "It is better to have one man die for the people than to have the whole nation destroyed."

From this telling statement rises the suspicion that the crisis of Palm Sunday is the crisis of every epoch and culture. We are torn between Christ and tribe, between casting our allegiance with him or with the nation, between the king's call and safety's comfort.

From Rwanda to Northern Ireland, from Bosnia to Guatemala City, from Johannesburg to Washington, the great contemporary struggle of faith is its clash with nationalism and tribalism. Under every moral crisis lurks a dread that if we ever fully followed Jesus, we would lose our holy privilege and our clannish protections. In Jesus' time, he was rejected and condemned for reasons of national security. So he is today.

So he was rejected throughout history—when Christianity seized the mighty throne of Europe, when missionaries blessed the search for gold and turned their shamed eyes away from torture, when good Christians prayed for their slaves, their just wars, their blessings of property and plunder.

Christians may not feel the full impact of Passion week because they fail to see that Jesus Christ is still betrayed for the sake of safe religion and imperious tribe or nation.

EASTER SUNDAY

20. The Easter Friends

Acts 10:34, 36–43; Col. 3:1–4; Jn. 20:1–18

"'Rabboni!' 'Do not cling to me.'"

How did Jesus love those he loved? Was there passion and warmth in his friendship? Was there ever the tinge of possessiveness and longing? Was he ever thrilled or rapt by the sight of friends? Did he need them?

He was a male. How did he relate to the "other," to women —not only his mother but those who were devoted and fond, those who cared and cherished, those who were drawn to him, and those who drew him near?

He had close friends, friends he wept for at Bethany, friends who wept over him. Peter, among his closest friends, remembers him fondly in his sermon at the house of Cornelius. Jesus healed. He went about doing good. He forgave. In other words, he loved.

His love lifted people up. His love healed their wounds. His love raised their hopes. His love exalted their spirits.

Among his friends, those he healed and raised in spirit, was Mary Magdalene—the image and model (in some traditions) of a love, once indiscriminate and disordered, now transformed and pure. It was Mary Magdalene who came to the tomb early in darkness, that first day of the week, and saw that he was gone. It was she who ran to the others, crying that they had taken the Lord away. Peter and John, old and dear friends as well, running to that tomb, must have felt the great rush of expectancy. How could they not burst with joy when they saw the absence of death, when they "saw" and then "believed."

Mary Magdalene, meanwhile, wept. As she wept, she saw two angels where the body had once been. Then, seeing but not recognizing Jesus, she heard from him the same words the angels had spoken, "Why are you weeping?" Kindled by some spark of hope or anger, she blurted out, "Tell me where you have put him and I will take him away." Despite the formality of these accounts, it is evident that there is a profound love and attachment between Christ and his friends.

"Mary."

"Teacher."

"Do not hold on to me, because I have not yet ascended. Go to my brothers and say to them, 'I am ascending to my Father and your Father, to my God and your God.'"

We Christians believe in an incarnate God, so incarnate that even after death, the body is promised preservation in its glory. The emotions, joys, attachments, and ecstasies of embodiment are themselves redeemed from being hostage to chains of space and time. For an Easter people, loves are never disembodied. A sheerly Platonic relation is impossible for us —even in heaven. It has been difficult at times for some

Christians to accept this, since they imagine a sexual or specifi-
cally genital agenda as the only alternative to disembodied
love. But the friends in Christ's own life and the stirring loves
of our great friendships show another way.

Christ, in his life and people, reveals a love that is full and
robust, intense and enduring, of which sexual union might be
one but not a necessary expression. The love that is promised
beyond our being born and dying is a love as deeply human as
it is transcendent. It moves the heart and dwells in the cham-
bers of eternity as well. So it was that St. Paul could write with
an ache of body and spirit to his Philippian friends: "You have
a permanent place in my heart, and God knows how much I
miss you all, loving you as Christ Jesus loves you."

21. The Trying of Faith

Acts 2:42–47; 1 Pt. 1:3–9; Jn. 20:1–9

"More precious than passing splendor."

The early Easter church of faith worked wonders. These believers performed signs, prayed, shared everything, heaped
generosity, worked hard every day, praised God, and won new
recruits. They even got along with each other, judging from
the accounts of the early parts of Acts. Later chapters, however,
prove that the long labor of faith was only beginning. It was
not all sweetness and light.

No doubt it is those rosy pictures of the first Christians that
dominate our minds when we think that, if we were really a
people of faith, everything would be hunky-dory. We "People
of God" would behave and perform far better than we seem to
be doing. We would also be more impressive, "winning the

approval of all" as the early church did. Well, we are not getting much approval—neither from the world around us nor from each other.

The same gap between expectation and performance gapes in our individual personal lives. One would think that we'd be doing marvels if we really had faith. There would not be so much confusion in our lives. We would not be contentious. We would pray more and hurt less. We would not be so haunted by doubts. We would be happy. We'd be nicer. Life would not be so daunting.

We presume that faith, like love, should make things easy, even effortless. We imagine that if we really believed in and loved God, we would, in the words of the First Letter of Peter, "rejoice with inexpressible joy." Love is supposed to feel good, at least so say the songs. And you'd think that faith would make things a little less arduous and more fulfilling.

I have now begun to think otherwise. The philosopher Immanuel Kant helped change my mind. His view of life is not very fashionable today, but that may be because we are in such a mess. We think something is drastically wrong if we feel unhappy or unfulfilled. Kant, on the other hand, thought that feeling good or being fulfilled had little or nothing to do with ethics and moral goodness. What counted for Kant was whether we were doing what we knew was right. Ease and inclination had nothing to do with it. After all, what really tests and shows the moral character of a person? Telling the truth when it is fulfilling and easy, or when it is difficult and daring? Where is the greater moral worth to be found? In a faithful spouse who enjoys being faithful, or in a faithful spouse who finds it difficult?

I don't mean to imply, even if Kant may have, that a thing is good only if it is painful. But there is a wisdom in seeing that there is more to goodness, love, and faith than the feeling of success or fulfillment that may accompany them. Perhaps a parent's greatest love for a child appears more in the hard times than the happy times. Perhaps a friend's trust in me is more deeply felt when inclination is otherwise than when it seems effortless.

What I am getting at is this: Admittedly, the delight, the "inexpressible joy," is part of Easter faith. But our faith in the risen Lord is revealed in sad and troubling moments as well.

The Twelve, remember, were locked in. They were in fear; there was a lack of peace; perhaps there was confusion, pain, and division. It is into that unsettled disquiet that Jesus came. Even then the Apostles were not able to experience fully the joy of his presence without entering the mystery of his wounds. Once they saw his hands and side, the remnants of pain and sorrow, they could rejoice.

The experience of faith is not the absence of pain or sorrow or loss. It is, rather, the bearing of pain or sorrow in faith. Faith does not take away the wounds; it transforms them. In faith, flaws are not obliterated; they are refined and purified.

Thomas, still hanging around a community of faith, discovers Christ in his unbelief. Although they kept telling Thomas —it went on for a week—that Jesus had risen, he refused to believe. "I'll not believe" without entering the wounds. How right he was. Faith must be found as much in the wounds of life as in the glories. And from the wounds a faith might most amazingly emerge. "My Lord and my God," that skeptic is reported to have said.

There is a subtext to Jesus' comment that while Thomas became a believer in the seeing, those who do not have the joy of seeing offer something far more splendid in their act of sightless faith. We are told that Jesus did other signs. The ones scripture records are meant to help us believe that Jesus is the Messiah. That belief, that faith, is finally felt and expressed not in sheer joy alone, but in arduous trial, in the plague of worry or doubt, in the grip of fear. These lacks, these wounds, these trials make faith shine all the more and the hearts that hold such faith more precious than gold.

"Through your faith, God's power will guard you. . . . This is a cause for great joy, even though you may for a short time have to bear being plagued by all sorts of trials; so that, when Jesus is revealed, your faith will have been tested and proved like gold—only it is more precious than gold, which is corruptible even though it bears testing by fire."

22. The Testing of Faith

Acts 2:14, 22–28; 1 Pt. 1:17–21; Lk. 24:13–35

"We were hoping that he was the one."

One of my favorite pictures—I have a copy of it pasted into my book for the Liturgy of the Hours—shows a scene of three robed figures walking along a dirt road, shafts of sun breaking through trees and clouds. The man in the middle, hand upraised as he talks, seems to fascinate the others. Ahead in the hazy distance is a town, perhaps Emmaus.

Although there are many other artistic renditions of the scene, this one appeals to me the most. The perspective allows the viewer to observe the travelers from behind. They are walking away from Jerusalem; and since they have yet to "recognize" him in the breaking of bread, they do not realize the Lord is with them.

It's a lovely Easter story that the Gospel of Luke gives us. Here we have two people who seem to think everything is over. They have just experienced a great loss. "We had hoped," they say, "he was the one to set Israel free." Not only have they left the community, they don't place much credence in the testimony of the women who heard angels declaring Jesus alive. Other witnesses saw the empty tomb, but not Jesus. Perhaps that is why they are walking away.

Observe what is going on here. We have two people who

seem to be in a situation of unbelief, hitting the road, leaving their community, deep in confusion. Two things happen. One, they are joined by Jesus on the road. He actually walks with them in their loss of hope and in their bewilderment. Two, he asks them to tell their story, and he stays to have dinner with them. Even when he chides them for their weak faith and goes through the scriptural promises of the messiah, they are not in a state of full belief. They have yet to recognize him. Only with the breaking of the bread are their eyes opened; and at that moment of recognition, he vanishes from sight.

Imagine this incident as a metaphor of how God deals with someone who has gone away or lost the way, an image of how we could deal with each other in our unbelief. With the breaking of the bread, the two wayfarers are brought into communion, even though they have not fully acknowledged the mystery that beckons them.

The story of the disciples on the road to Emmaus presents a strange state of affairs indeed. Jesus was more with them on their journey, even in their doubt and unbelief, than when they actually saw and recognized him and finally believed. And it was only in retrospect that they could see that their hearts were enkindled as they were walking and talking on the road—even though they did not know that it was he who was explaining the scriptures to them.

I find this paradox of faith, of distance and closeness, of belief and unbelief, repeated over and over again in people's lives. Although I cannot see when or if it happens to me, it is startlingly clear when I witness it in others.

A man tells me he feels distant from God. He is unhappy about the sense of separation. He regrets his carelessness with the gifts that have been given him, the loves entrusted to him. He wishes he were more attentive, more "close" to God, more appreciative and prayerful. Finally, and strangely, there are times when he wonders whether he trusts in God at all. In those times he feels at sea, at a loss.

A young, vibrant woman wonders if she has lost her faith.

She doesn't feel its magic anymore. She only wishes she could have back those moments when it all felt so wonderful. Now it just seems empty without God. I ask her: "Well, do you believe in God the creator and father of Jesus Christ your savior?" "Oh yes." "Do you believe that Jesus died for you and is risen with a promise for you of eternal life?" "Of course; but I don't feel it. I miss having a relationship with God."

Now look at these people and imagine you are God. One is sad only because he misses you, because he takes you for granted; and his worst times are when he thinks you might not exist. He finds the thought of your nonexistence almost unbearable.

The young woman says that life feels empty without you. She only wishes she could feel your presence more, that she could see and talk with you again. Her greatest worry is that she might have lost her faith in you.

Now, do you, God, think you have a relationship with them? Do you think they have a relationship with you? Do you think they love you? Do you think they hope and trust in you? Is not their whole life, their whole being, a prayer?

"We had hoped," they said on the road to Emmaus. Once there was hope, they thought. But even their sense of loss, their longing for the hope, was hope. Even their desire to believe was believing. Even their longing to love was love.

And so, present with him at the table, they finally recognized the gift of the presence that was there all along, walking away, talking away, wondering why, telling their woe, hearing his story once again.

Finally recognizing him, they set their faces toward Jerusalem to tell the others how their hearts were set on fire, not only in the breaking of the bread, but when he revealed to them their past and future glory.

It all happened on the road.

23. The Sheepgate

Acts 2:14, 36–41; 1 Pt. 2:20–25; Jn. 10:1–10

"I lay down my life."

"Over my dead body!" Have you ever heard that challenge? It seems to bang around in my brain as something I've surely heard a few times and maybe even said. These words push their way back into my consciousness when I see this Sunday's readings.

It is not so much the content of Peter's ringing sermon in the Acts of the Apostles that triggers the words. It is rather the First Letter of Peter, with its daunting description of Christ and the manner of his suffering that bring "over my dead body" to mind. We are told that Christ's suffering is a path for us to follow. And yet it remains, for the most part, truly a "road not taken" by people and institutions that bear the name of Christ.

"He did no wrong; no deceit was found in his mouth. When he was insulted he returned no insult. When he was made to suffer, he did not counter with threats. No, he delivered himself up to the one who judges justly. In his own body, he brought your sins to the cross, so that all of us, dead to sin, could live in accord with God's will. By his wounds you were healed."

This is hard bread to chew. We think that if we do no wrong and tell no lies, we have some justice due us. We might have the gumption to take insults without retaliation, but to undergo pain and suffering and offer no resistance—that is too much to expect. Jesus, for his part, does not rely on his innocence or righteousness or the truth of his ideas. His sole security is the one who sent him.

More troubling still, Jesus takes our sin into his own body

on the cross. Only by his wounds and death are we healed and given life. It is over his dead body that we are saved.

That is what this letter seems to be saying. How proper, then, that the next few words allude to the fact that we were like straying sheep who are now returned to our shepherd, the guardian of our souls.

The Good Shepherd, as we all know, is one of the abiding pictures of Christ in Christian imagination. Words like "pastor" and "pastoral care" draw their meaning and power from the image of Jesus as the kind and caring guide of the flock. The sheep approach the protection of the sheepfold through the gate. Those who climb in by other ways—over the rocks and brambles—are either robbers or predators. The true shepherd enters and leaves first, calling their names; at the sound of his voice they follow.

This passage is called a "figure" by the writer of the Fourth Gospel. And when the hearers seem not to grasp the figure fully, Jesus goes further, offering them what many have thought a somewhat disconnected second metaphor. All of a sudden, he is no longer the shepherd. He is the gate itself.

But this shift is not a mixing of metaphors. Like many devoted shepherds, Jesus is both the shepherd and the gate.

I once heard a description of Middle Eastern sheepherding practices that ties these two images together. The sheepfold, especially one unattached to a larger settlement or dwelling, is a circular wall of stones, topped by barriers of briar. There is a small opening for the sheep to pass through. Once they are all in, instead of closing a hinged gate, the shepherd simply lies across the opening, so that nothing or no one can get through without going over his body first, without confronting or even killing him. This particular kind of shepherd literally makes himself into a barrier gate, a role that requires not only care but courage. If any marauders or predators are to get to the sheep, they will only do so over the dead body of the shepherd.

When Jesus reveals that he is the gate of the sheepfold, he is not just suggesting that he is the unique way into safety or the only way out to pasture. He is saying that he will prevent our destruction by laying down his life. He has come to us that we may have life and have it abundantly.

The continuation of the passage is important. "I am the good shepherd, the one that lays down his life for the sheep." It is for this reason, we are assured, that God's love is so totally poured out into Christ—and so empowering that his life, even though laid down, is given back again.

The Passover, with its commemoration of Christ's "dead body" and Resurrection, is the full realization of the twenty-third Psalm's promise. With this shepherd, we shall never want. We will have repose. We will be led and refreshed and guided along right paths.

"Even in the dark valley I will fear no evil. You are at my side. You give me courage. You are my food and drink. You anoint me. There is nothing I shall want. Goodness and kindness will follow me all my days. I will dwell in your fold forever."

Can we be lost or destroyed? Only over the Lord's dead body. But he is risen now, to die no more. Through the laying down of his life on the cross and his rising before us, we are led into the sheepfold of eternal life.

FIFTH SUNDAY OF EASTER

24. Deacons

Acts 6:1–7; 1 Pt. 2:4–9; Jn. 14:1–12

"We shall appoint them to this task."

The appointment of deacons, as recounted in the Acts of the Apostles, was a response to the needs of fellow Christians and the desires of the Twelve to be more available for prayer and the proclamation of the word.

While the task at hand concerned material requirements of the community—the fair distribution of food among the widows—what is more interesting about the account is the Apostles' flexibility in responding to the needs of their time.

As the ages rolled by, the function and meaning of the diaconate took various shapes, sometimes of minor importance, but always linked to service, whether liturgical or communal. In the contemporary Western church, the hallmark of deacons is that they assist, not preside, even though, in response to need, deacons do preside at baptisms, marriages, and burials. Thus, the diaconate gets more closely linked to the priesthood. But I hope not too close.

I have often wondered whether there is a hidden hindrance in the preaching and the hearing of the word in today's Catholicism. I mean more than the quality and length of sermons. It is inevitable that some of us preachers are just not as good as others—certainly not as good as some preachers who have grown up more in the tradition of the word than of sacrament.

There is a deeper issue here that involves our lives and labors. As an old African-American woman told a group of us one day, "I'd rather hear one sermon lived than ten preached."

If there are problems with our preaching, it is not only that we are too busy doing other things—although administrative duties can consume a pastor in any parish. A far bigger problem is this: even the best of homilies can be sloughed off because it is tied to the very nature of the presiding office, the task, the business of priestcraft.

A significant charism of deacons in the contemporary church is related to the fact that most of them are married, have other places of work, have had an active career, and have no reason to give service to the church other than their faith. The work of priests, even their preaching, can be subconsciously passed off as "what they have to do." But when a deacon visits the sick, when a mail carrier or a business person gets into the pulpit, something else is going on. And people know this. It is not just "their job."

There is something particularly moving and engaging about an ordinary person who wants to read and preach the word of God—and it's not "business as usual." It can't be sloughed off as something that is "expected" to be done. The witness of married folk, living "ordinary" lives, is most powerful precisely because they do not need to do it, nor are they expected to do so. One of the charisms of the Promise-Keepers and Opus Dei is the fact that people who seem ordinary desire to do uncommon things for God and community. Similarly, the primary source of vocations to the priesthood or conversions to the Catholic faith is the example of family members, friends, and co-workers. It is a matter of persons, not institutional strategy.

Two of my closest friends, till the day they died, had prayed for the ordination of women in the Catholic church. Though they are gone, I still hold their hope that if it is the will of God and the work of the Spirit, the church will have the humility to change.

Yet both of these women eventually confided to me that they experienced in their labors (one as a nun-physician, the other as a wife and professional photographer) strange powers of communicating faith that no priest or preacher seemed to have. Since they didn't have to preach and pray, people could not ignore them the way they could ignore an official minister. Since they were not expected to be servants of the poor, advocates for justice, or ministers of the word, they could not easily be explained away.

This is the very thing I experienced in those moments when married women scouted the far reaches of mystical prayer or a father of a large family revealed before me and other men how his life would have no final meaning or joy without Christ. We have all known deacons who, because of their kind service, led others to say, "See how those Catholics love one another—and others as well." It was precisely because they were not priests that they were so effective.

We are a chosen race, a royal priesthood, a consecrated

nation. The ritual prayer that commissions deacons should be for us all. "Receive the Gospel of Christ whose herald you are; believe what you read, preach what you believe, put into practice what you preach."

Whatever our office in the church, we are all called to be deacons, just as we are called to the priesthood of faithful believers. The diversity of roles is life-giving. A mother lives what I could never preach. A celibate reveals a color in the spectrum of faith that spouses cannot. A single lay person consoles in ways that other Christians never could.

Is it not appropriate, then, that Jesus is reported to have said, "In my father's house there are many mansions"?

25. Baptism in the Spirit

Acts 8:5–8, 14–17; 1 Pt. 3:15–18; Jn. 14:15–21

"There was great joy in that city."

Some Catholic parents experience the sadness of seeing their children, once they reach or pass adolescence, leave the church of their childhood. I have never encountered a response of indifference to this among parents. Rather, their feelings and faith span a range from anger, through guilt and worry, to an abiding trust in God and their children as well.

Although watching one's children drift into a churchless way of life can be a jolt, it seems to be even more unsettling to some mothers and fathers to see their child leave Catholicism for something "better." A son or daughter undergoes a conversion experience, is "baptized in the Spirit," or finds deep Christian fellowship somewhere else.

I have yet to discover a satisfying account of how this happens. One thing is sure: there are no guaranteed causes of

faith or its loss. Some children with casually Catholic upbring-
ings become devoted churchgoers as adults. Others with a
strict and extensive exposure to the traditions and practices of
the church reject it all. Our example, the environment of the
home, the culture at large, the range of education, the quality
of friendships—all influence the formation of a committed
Catholic adult, but all of them together cannot ensure it.

What if a teenager discovers a new life of faith, prayer, and
commitment in a Christian community other than ours? A
number of times I have been approached by young adults who
have had such an experience. To each person I put the
following questions: Does it lead you into deeper union with
Christ? Does it foster a life of greater virtue and service? Does
it increase your faith, hope, and charity?

If the answers are yes, I then talk about the unique grace
and goodness, as well as the deficiencies, of Catholicism; and
if our young ones are not tempted to reject this faith of ours,
given through our church and sacraments, I bless their
journey and entrust it to God.

Is that heresy? Should a strong and stern warning be given?
If this were done, would it have any effect? Would a life of
tepid or cafeteria-style Catholicism be better? To be sure, luke-
warmness is not a universal trait of Catholics; but we do have
to admit that there are lacks in our church. Maybe we neglect
some of the emotive power, the courage, the unique feeling of
faith that is appropriate for a people truly saved by Christ and
baptized in his Spirit. Our faith, one would think, is meant to
be engaging and transforming.

Certainly, to judge by the accounts in the Acts of the
Apostles, Philip's proclamation of the Messiah manifested such
power that the whole town of Samaria felt a joy described as at
"fever pitch." After accepting the Word of God, Peter and John
met with them to pray that they might receive the Holy Spirit.
Do we pray with and for our own young in such a manner?

Beyond baptism in the name of the Lord Jesus, the Apostles
also imposed hands on the new believers so that they might

receive the Holy Spirit. In our own preparation for the sacrament of confirmation, many parishes seem to be increasingly aware of the opportunity to invite our young into a mature commitment and courageous conviction.

Apparently it was such conviction that led to the heroic examples of suffering for the name of Christ to which the First Letter of Peter alludes.

In any event, in the Fourth Gospel Jesus does promise a Paraclete, a Spirit of truth that the world does not see or accept. Are we ourselves so comfortable with our world and its language that our children judge our faith to be neither profound nor special? The Spirit that Christ promised would be revealed by a life of love. Is that the Spirit our young hunger for?

For our part, we might learn more deeply that our faith engages feeling as well as reason and practicality, that it involves not only practices and creed, but a personal relationship to Christ. We might ask if we really care enough about our faith that we desire to bestow it as our dearest gift to our young. Perhaps it is then that we will have experienced greater fellowship and solidarity as well as a sense of Catholic uniqueness.

The Spirit of Christ is the bearer of a mighty truth that challenges the world and transforms our hearts. We are called to lives of holy resistance and revolution. We really do offer something different and most strategic to the world. If we believe that, how could we not want to talk of faith and proclaim Jesus as our Messiah?

As for those young people who might leave us, the last chapter is not yet written for their lives. Just as our church itself has a long and winding history, so do the great majority of its communicants. Through it all, what is most important is that the believer, as well as the believing community, pass on to its young the great truth that Jesus Christ has saved us. Such is the ground of our faith and hope as well as of all the Spirit's gifts. That is why it is only into God's hands that we entrust our lives—and the lives of those we love.

26. The Beyond

Acts 1:12–14; 1 Pt. 4:13–16; Jn. 17:1–11

"Jesus looked up to heaven."

Jesus had a good season this Eastertide. During Holy Week he made the covers of *Time, Newsweek,* and *U.S. News and World Report*—a phenomenon that might lead us to think that he had really changed the world for good, except for the fact that the Unabomber appeared on all three covers the following week.

Anyway, the three magazines vary greatly in their knowledge about Jesus. The real superstars of the articles are speculative theoreticians, whose own imaginings and desires we find in abundance.

Robert Funk, who started the Jesus Seminar and has taught at the academic shrines of Texas, Harvard, and Emory, wants to "set Jesus free," he says, from scripture and creed.

But what, one might ask, is left of Jesus Christ without scripture, without creed? Well, he's more like a "Jewish Socrates or Lenny Bruce," we are told: "Jesus was perhaps the first stand-up comic"—not political, not programmatic, offering no program for the world. It turns out that the most reliable description of Jesus is that he is "an ironic secular sage."

Some theoreticians say that Jesus is a projection of Christian need and faith. Isn't it strange, then, how like a professor their Jesus is, this "ironic secular sage"? 'Tis a pity he himself was not tenured, that he was not interviewed by one of the more reputable reporters of his time, that he had not published in a peer-reviewed journal.

I do not mean to belittle or caricature the contemporary academic readings of Jesus Christ. Surely there is a rich diversity of opinion and quality in the theologians quoted by our newsweeklies. There is also devoted and painstaking research going on in our universities.

But the media coverage merits a clear and critical look. The cover stories of our magazines represent a religious crisis of our times: not just the refusal to face up to the crucifixion and Resurrection of Jesus Christ, but a deep resistance to the transcendent God whom Jesus reveals.

How close is the so-called contemporary account of Jesus to a rejection of any faith in a God beyond? What criteria are used? All miracles must be deemed impossible; any mention of transcendence is suspect; all messianic claims, all reference to an afterlife are unacceptable; any thought that we need salvation by his death on a cross must be repressed.

The contemporary "secular sage" insists that it is all so ordinary, this faith, this story, this gospel, this Jesus. Yet it is precisely the extraordinary, the supernatural, that makes him what he is—not only his moral teachings (which some great sage might dream up), but also his resurrected body (which no other religion has come up with), and the seeming disgrace of his cross. No human inventiveness would dare to concoct what was an embarrassment to the Roman Empire, a stumbling block to the Greek world, and a repudiation of Gnosticism. As the luminous Kierkegaard suggested, if faith is an offense to rationality, how might reason deal with faith other than by rejecting it?

It is not new, this struggle of faith in Jesus Christ. Since the beginning it was known that if we banish Christ's divinity, he and all of us are utterly alone. He was just another heap of chemicals who died. It is humanity alone on that cross. And it is a stranded humanity that is left with post-Resurrection delusions.

But if we believe that Jesus is indeed the eternal Word of God made flesh, then our very God was crucified as well; and the destiny of our dying bodies is somehow found in the presence of the almighty God.

If we do not believe that the cross bore the sorrows of God as much as it does our own, we ought not to have approached that wood to kneel. If we do not believe that by his Resurrection we are destined to be free, we ought not to have sung our alleluias on his day of victory. If it was not a heavenly, unearthly Jerusalem to which Jesus ascended, we ought not gather to look and pray to a God beyond who beckons us.

For it is sheer folly, the things we have done this Paschal season, if Christ does not reveal our sublime fortune. It was all a charade if our saving God was not on that cross, if it was not miraculously one of us who ascended on high. But if we worshiped in faith this season, we have again professed that, rather than being dupes of folly, we are the agents of the only true revolution that has graced human history.

In the death, resurrection, and ascension of Jesus, neither Christ nor we are "confined" to dogma or scripture. Rather, our God is revealed and we are therein liberated.

It is God-with-us, Emmanuel, who died our death. It is the God who called history forth and loved it enough to marry it, to preserve and save it, to redeem its terrible, fragile beauty. Thus it was with full heart that we could pray: "We adore thee, O Christ, and we bless thee, because by thy holy cross thou hast redeemed the world." And it is with faith in the miraculous, the transcendent, that we, like Jesus in the Fourth Gospel, look to heaven for the giver of eternal life, the glory of the earth and the love and truth from which we all came.

PENTECOST

27. The Church of Many Voices

Acts 2:1–11; 1 Cor. 12:3–7, 12–13; Jn. 20:19–23

"What the Spirit brings is very different."

There are many gifts in the church, many ministries, many works, many members. That's a problem. Who's best? Who's important? Who has the right way? Who corners the truth?

Some of us would love to have the special charism of solitary prayer. But not having it, we might think ourselves inferior. More distressing, we might envy contemplatives or even resort to the tactic of thinking that prayer isn't so special after all. (Those people who run from the world, hide in their rooms, frequent chapels: wouldn't it be better if they were like us, finding God in the rough and tumble, helping the poor, being busy?)

Then again, others of us wish we had the charism of community: family, relationships, friends, parties, gatherings. Social stars shine. They seem to engage others effortlessly. How do those people manage to be so outgoing and open? The same hints of our inferiority, however, set us on the way to envy and then resentment. (They're nothing but enthusiasts, extroverts with slick surface and little depth. They usually are the ones who don't care about peace and justice, as long as they are having a good time.)

Many of us, in our better moments, admire Christian social activists—people who hunger, thirst, and labor for justice. In our worse moments, however, we wish they wouldn't bother us or remind us that the gospels challenge our way of life. (These people ought to get their own act together instead of trying to change the world. After all, we can't hope for heaven on earth. All they do is send us on guilt trips.)

Surely those who have devoted their lives to the corporal works of mercy win the respect of us all. Has there ever been a time when we did not secretly desire to be like them? But this desire, too, sometimes sours; and the example of "do-gooders" feels more like a rebuke than an inspiration. (Bleeding hearts. Why do they care only about the poor—and not the rest of us? At least they could take better care of their own kin. Even that Mother Teresa, she only did band-aid work, anyway. Why didn't she challenge the unjust political and economic structures?)

These examples, of course, are just caricatures; but they do suggest attitudes that stir hostility and division in the church. One might wonder, for example, whether some of the sharp quarrels between liberal and conservative, right and left, traditionalist and reformist are more a function of particularism and resentment than they are expressions of profound faith.

Are there not gifts of conservatives that liberals miss? Isn't there a ministry the liberal gives us that the conservative does not? Do not traditionalists as well as innovators have a charism? Don't contemplatives, social activists, Catholic Workers, and urban families all embody our faith in ways both necessary and complementary?

St. Paul, I propose, would say yes. The variety of talents and works, whether of Jew or Greek, slave or free, serves the common good. The diversity of the members makes them a body. But to be one body, they must have one Spirit and speak with one voice. "Jesus is Lord," is their fundamental message, announced by those who drink of the same Spirit.

This is the Spirit that on Pentecost filled the disciples. It was so strong a confirmation of faith in Jesus that believers could speak in a way that was not only united but was universally understood. This is the Spirit that Jesus, in John's Gospel, breathes in a moment of peace, igniting discipleship.

It is the Spirit, as the great hymn "Veni Sancte Spiritus" recalls, which inhabits the heart of the poor as well as the solitary. It quickens joy, eases sorrow. It permeates deep intelligence as well as high feeling. It transforms labor as well as the human heart.

In the Letter to the Galatians we read that, as opposed to sexual indulgence, idolatry, wrangling, jealousy, ill-temper, disagreements, factions, envy, and orgy, "what this Spirit brings is different: love, joy, peace, trustfulness, kindness, goodness, gentleness, patience, and self-control."

What a wonder it would be, what a breeze of life, what a fire of zeal, if differences in the church were marked by these gifts of Pentecost. Rather than all our particular ideologies, our special interests, our private fixations, we would communicate to the world (and to the young) in a language that we all understand. It is the language of the Holy Spirit, the language of love, revealed in patience and kindness, generosity and trust, and a faith both forgiving and enduring.

What a gift to speak the language of such love. What a renewal of the earth as well as our church. Rather than being shamed by the grace of another, we would be graced. Rather than shrink at comparisons, we arise in praise to God.

Is such a gift worth praying for? The alleluia verse of Pentecost leaves no doubt: "Come, Holy Spirit, fill the hearts of your faithful; and kindle in them the fire of your love."

TRINITY SUNDAY

28. In the Name of the Father

Ex. 34:4–6, 8–9; 2 Cor. 13:11–13; Jn. 3:16–18

"Grace, love, and fellowship."

June is traditionally the month to honor the Holy Trinity. It is also, in the United States, the month when fathers are honored. That's an opportune, if delicate, congruence.

I have friends, some men but especially women, who have

found it difficult to pray to God as father. The reasons range from the psychological burden of a tyrannical parent to the theological reservation that fatherhood excludes the feminine-maternal in God and suggests the possibility that God is some one-sided initiator, a non-needer who started it all and then exited, indifferent to the drama.

To be sure, there is maternity in God. John Paul I, in his short papacy, reminded us that God is not only a father to us, but a mother as well. No doubt he was inspired by passages from the prophets and psalms or feminine references to the Spirit and Wisdom.

But what can be learned, no matter what our culture or history, from the fact that Jesus called God "Father" and that Christians have for centuries praised God in hymn and creed as Father, Son, and Spirit in Trinity?

Despite what the word "God" has meant to various times and cultures—remote creator, unfeeling authority, arbitrary ruler, or a clan of super-beings—in Christianity God is a community of persons. Mutuality is the source of life. Relationship grounds being. There is otherness from the start. The doctrine of the Trinity affirms God as loving and knowing, giving and receiving. We profess that God could not be God without the "other" (the Son) and the eternal bond of their relationship (the Spirit).

While some may think that the doctrine of the Trinity is negotiable, it is actually central to our faith. If we lose it, we lose all we are. Moses' personal God, "merciful and gracious, slow to anger, rich in kindness and fidelity," emerges in St. Paul as the interpersonal Trinity that models true human relationship. Thus Paul prays: "The grace of the Lord Jesus Christ, the love of God and the fellowship of the Spirit be with you all."

Jesus said to Nicodemus: "Yes, God so loved the world that he gave his only son to save the world." Our God, in love for us, offers the dearest—the Son—to be one with us, as one in Trinity. Jesus reveals something not only about God, but about fatherhood. It is an intimate, self-giving relationship.

I wonder if the "Father" of the Trinity is more strategic for humanity than it is for the Trinity? Our problem may not lie so much in what we assign to God as in what many people associate with failed fatherhood.

In our own time we hear of uncaring and abusing fathers, "dead-beat, absent dads," and "fatherless kids." The lost father is lost relationship, broken promise, torn covenant, lost Trinity. The disappearance of fatherhood is the disappearance of intimacy. But Jesus' father, nurturing and abiding, comforting and faithful, is radically different, and it would be most unfortunate if we were to ignore his revelation. We desperately need this father, strangely so like a mother.

When parenthood is true, its grace is as deep as it is divine. We are held in being with the other—spouse, father, and mother. How like the Trinity our covenants can be.

29. The Church of Unity

Dt. 8:2–3, 14–16; 1 Cor. 10:16–17; Jn. 6:51–58

"One bread, one body."

Moses instructed his people to remember how their God worked great wonders for them, brought them together, led them through the desert, fed them with a bread from heaven, freed them from slavery, and guided them through vast and dangerous lands.

So it is that we who call ourselves a "new Israel" might recall as well. What brought us together? What has been our journey? What has led us through the desert and given us food and drink? What liberates us? These are the questions of our unity—our history, our sustenance, our common faith.

The celebration of diversity sounds throughout our communities these days, from Boston and San Diego to Beirut and Santiago. But what keeps us together? What is the cohesion and unity that gives flesh and blood to our faith? If there is nothing that unifies us, what is the point of diversity?

Our body is Jesus Christ. Our source of unity is not Europe or America, not liberal or conservative, not charism or tradition, not white or colored pigment, not male or female, not papist or evangelical. It is Christ.

Corpus Christi, the body and blood of Christ, is the marriage of God and us. This union took place not only in the Incarnation; it is re-enacted in our Eucharists, whereby God in Christ is made one with our very flesh, the living sign that God is with and for us now and always.

"I am the living bread come down from heaven. Whoever eats this bread shall live forever; the bread I give is my flesh for the life of the world." For Christians there can be no life, if their life is not in Christ.

We often wonder: is there anything that is required of us to call ourselves Catholic, Christian? There is. To deny Christ is to deny our union. To deny that he is the very Word of God made flesh is to deny what we are. To deny that his death and Resurrection have saved us is to reject our cohesion. And to deny his real presence in our prayer together—especially our eucharistic prayer—is to reject our history and common identity.

We may be beset by sin or ignorance. We may fall short of what Christ has called us to. We may be confused by teachings or confounded by canon law, but we remain part of his body. If our particularity is all we have, if we think our individual lives are closed in upon themselves with their own isolated growth apart from the body of Christ, we develop cancerously, like separated and selfish cells.

But if the Eucharist is the celebration of our unity, it is our remembrance, our being re-membered, put back together as one body in Jesus Christ who shared our flesh and blood. Our solidarity in this faith is greater than all our differences when we partake of one food and drink to nourish us on our way.

Our Communion lines to the altars of the world have all

the splendor of tribes and customs, colors and song, classes and age. But they are processions to the one great gift we share. For this reason does the refrain of Father John Foley's majestic hymn of unity ring true:

> One bread, one body,
> one Lord of all;
> one cup of blessing
> which we bless;
> and we, though many
> throughout the earth,
> we are one body
> in this one Lord.

30. Only in God

Is. 49:14–15; 1 Cor. 4:1–5; Mt. 6:24–34

"I will never forget you."

In Israel's godforsakenness, she is reminded, "Can a mother be without tenderness for the child of her womb?" The unthinkable would have to happen before Israel could be lost or forgotten.

This demand for total reliance is echoed in St. Paul's placement of his destiny in the judgment of God alone. The prophet and the apostle have only one security. They have given themselves to only one master. Undivided hearts, they inhabit a world of faith where one lives without fear.

And so it was that Jesus told us that we could never serve two masters. There can be only one bottom line: not money and all it symbolizes of security or attainment, but the will of God.

The lovely Sermon on the Mount passage evoking the birds

of the air and the lilies of the field is actually a harrowing call to trust. It is a deficiency of faith that causes us to worry over health or food, past or future. The words are written easily enough, but the living of them is a daunting task. It is one thing to sing of trust in God; it is another to go through a CAT scan.

The composer John Foley has set this day's memorable Psalm 62 to a melody which draws us deeper and deeper into the purifying mystery of radical trust. When I have played his music for others in retreat or recollection, I have put the words into the more direct second person so we might feel its immediacy and risk:

> Only in God will my soul be at rest,
> From You comes my hope, my salvation.
> You alone are my rock of safety
> My strength, my glory, my God.

As each verse unfolds, I ask the singing congregation to confront the fears that hound us.

When we look into our interior lives, what causes us unrest? Our failings and disappointments so easily unsettle us. The sense that we are passed over or unappreciated casts us down. The threat of ill health or helplessness can freeze us in fear. Our value worries us. Do we make any difference at all? Do we count? In all these movements of our soul there is a persistent refrain. Where is our anchor, what do we rely on?

> Trust in God at all times, O people, and show forth your strength.

Perhaps we manage with these private worries, but are we to entrust God with all our relationships as well? That's another story. How often the loves we cling to are stifled by our fear of losing them. Our children feel our worries more readily than the care that fuels them. Past hurts settle into our hearts like clinkers. We are burdened with the people that want us and even more so by the people who seem not to. We alternately complain that we are too alone and too crowded. And it is precisely at these times that we find it so difficult to turn to the source of all love for consolation.

Many times have I heard you tell of your long-lasting love.

Even if, however, we manage to entrust ourselves and our loved ones into the hands of God, our social and political world can fill us with dread. Some worry for the future of the church: it is so rigid, it is so lax. Others stew over the state of the nation: so proud, brought so low. Many are alarmed at the condition of the world: so divided, so monolithic. Who or what can solve the latest crisis? Where can one turn?

Well, indeed our labors and efforts count in some way. But here as in every arena of life, there is no ultimate solution that is outside the hands of God.

God alone is a refuge for us and a stronghold for our fears.

In all things, what is our rock, what is our hope, what is our safety, what is our strength? And in all things, the answer bears a person's name, the only person who can serve as our security without becoming an idol that enslaves us in fear.

31. Orthopraxis

Dt. 11:18, 26–28; Rom. 3:21–25, 28; Mt. 7:21–27

"Put them into practice."

Perhaps the age-old argument about faith and good works will never end. After all, each side makes a good case for itself.

There should be no pretense that we mere humans could save ourselves or that somehow our achievements, our works, could insure our deliverance. The annals of the world and the behavior of the tribes and nations, even those most abundant and sophisticated, shatter any illusion that we are not, as Paul writes, "sinners deprived of the glory of God." It is only by the justification by God through our faith in Jesus, we are told, that we get the undeserved gift of redemption.

And yet faith seems something much more than the simple recognition and acceptance of God. Moses wanted his people to take his words into their very hearts and souls. "Bind them at your wrist as a sign, and let them be a pendant on your forehead." They must obey the commandments. They must live the truth.

Surely this is what Jesus is getting at when he warns his disciples that the plea, "Lord, Lord," is not an assurance of heaven. *Doing* the will of God, not just knowing or accepting it, is required of us. Neither prophecies nor miracles serve as guarantees of salvation. It is not just the hearing or preaching of the Word which is required of us; it is the practicing of it which builds our house on solid ground.

There is no question that such a passage has led people to believe that it is their own actions which bring about salvation. The Pelagian heresy seems almost part of the human genome.

But its mirror image, a magical belief in words and dogmas

that leads to a strange quietism, haunts the double helix as well.

The exclusive concentration on orthodoxy can take at least two forms. First, we must say the right words to be saved. These words may be "I'm sorry," "I'm saved," or "Lord, Lord." Or second, we must hold the right beliefs to be saved. These are the core truths, the central dogma, the received teaching.

Neither of these orthodoxies is enough. Without the living, the embodiment, of faith in action, words and dogmas are actually empty. For faith is not merely a matter of knowing some truth or saying it. It is, rather, believing in a person whom we allow to transform our lives.

Our actions, our prayers, our good works may not bring about our redemption. But they are, indeed, the fruit of a faith taken seriously, "bound to our wrists" and "written on our faces" in such a way that we have not only heard the Good News, we live it. The living out of our faith is the actual building of it on the rock of faith who is the revealing Christ of God. It is only when we let the revelation take hold in our real lives that we will find our faith standing firm before the winds and torrents of life.

This is not just orthodoxy. It is orthopraxis.

32. What God Really Wants

Hos. 6:3–6; Rom. 4:18–25; Mt. 9:9–13

"It is love that I desire . . . and knowledge of God."

There is a secret and deadly craving I have now and then. I discover it usually when I feel either like a dismal failure or a happy success. What unites these disparate frames of mind is a shared ambition that I might present myself to the crucified

Lord and tell him I didn't need his trouble, or that I wasn't worth it.

"These other people need your salvation, but I'm in pretty good shape. I've grown in the virtues, made sacrifices, been to confession, and received the sacrament of the sick."

When I'm down, however, the monologue goes a little differently. "Well maybe the others are worthy, but not me. I've grown more tepid and self-centered, squandered opportunities, and maybe don't even know the evil I've done."

The common theme here is that being healthy before God has become so important that when I'm healthy, I see no need, and when I'm unhealthy, I think I am beyond cure.

The first posture is that of the Pharisee (not the historical class, necessarily, but a particular image in the gospel) in me. When I'm in this mode, performance and credit mean a lot—what I've done, what I've failed to do. I slip very easily into comparisons here. "Well, at least I'm not as bad as he, as foolish as she." At its worst, looking down on everyone else, I become a stern admonitor, even a judge. I become adept at criticizing the best of people, and sometimes people I don't even know who walk past me in an airport.

Paul wrote that what is credited to us is not accomplishments but our faith in Jesus and the love that such faith elicits. It is hard to accept this if you feel self-righteous. Perhaps this is why Jesus found it easy to call tax collectors and sinners. They, at least, knew that they could not do it on their own. They had felt the failure. They had known the need and were grateful. "It is mercy I desire, not sacrifices." Do we misunderstand what God wants of us if we think our sin—the absence or presence of it—is more significant than God's kind grace? Are we wrong when we think our performance is more important than our presence?

I have wondered more than once whether God is somehow like the late Father Bill Parsons. After a long life of service, he was felled by a stroke. A brother Jesuit, my community superior, was especially devoted to Father Bill and visited him frequently.

"I wish I knew what Bill wanted, but I can't make out what he's saying. He just gets out 'I . . . waaa . . . you. . . .' I'm always trying to guess. Do you want to walk? Go for a ride? Get rest? Have a beer? Bill just shakes his head in frustration; then I pick out something to do for him and hope it's what he wants."

Well, one day my friend Tom came home all excited. He couldn't wait to tell me that he finally found out what Father Bill was wanting.

He was saying, "I . . . waaa . . . ove . . . you."

33. The Great Harvest

Ex. 19:2–6; Rom. 5:6–11; Mt. 9:36–10:8

"The gift you have received, give as a gift."

We spend our lives waiting for the harvest—that moment when we will taste the fruit of our labor. The wait, however, seems endless.

Once we got to high school, we may have thought harvest-time was close by, the time to be all we had wanted to be, to do all we had planned. Then, high school gone, we awaited the day of university graduation, marriage, or religious profession. We jumped through hoops, passed exams, made promises, applied for jobs. Surely the time had come for bearing fruit and savoring it.

Finished with our schooling, unless we sought more preparation as pre-professionals or pre-professors, we thought that with marriage or some other commitment, we would finally be what we had been becoming.

Marriageables married, pre-professionals professed, would-be religious became such. Yet "someday" still described the harvest.

Someday. Once I have kids. Once I make vows. Once I get hired. Once I have a final assignment. Then. Then I will do it. Then I will live. Then I will reap the harvest.

For those who marry, there may be further postponement. The harvest will come when children are born, when they are all in school, when they finally get out of school, when they are married or have jobs. Then the time for savoring will arrive.

If we are single or in community life, we begin to suspect that only with retirement will we reap the harvest.

Retirement comes. And what do we do? We do what we have learned and practiced. We wait. We postpone once again. What we have learned is how not to harvest.

Jesus, seeing us tired and exhausted, was moved with pity. "The harvest is good, but laborers are scarce. Beg the harvester to send laborers to gather the harvest."

It is all ready to be reaped, this life, this labor, the upshot of our plans and planting. It is all here. But we continue to work at postponement, not the reaping.

The task of healing wounds can begin right now. The walking dead—those who think there is no point, no promise, no possibility—can be summoned from their tombs. Others, hidden like lepers of old, outcast and undesired not only in distant countries, but in our towns, our parishes, our homes, await our welcome.

The spells cast on our children, obsessed with trinkets and possessed by illusions, are ready to be broken. Sly demons even today fear rebuke, dispersion, and disarmament.

How is it done? Not by postponement, but by active loving, here and now. Each person before us is somehow our special care. Each moment is opportune.

The love we harvest is not a *quid pro quo* thing or a nonrenewable natural resource. It grows and flowers in our giving of it. It is like the gift of Jesus recalled in the Letter to the Romans: unmerited yet freely offered in a life laid down for one's friends.

We yield love any time, any place we labor at it. Life itself is but a field ripe with opportunity. The task we have as love's disciples is to harvest it.

34. Providence

Jer. 20:10–13; Rom. 5:12–15; Mt. 10:26–33

"Do not be afraid of them."

The objects of our fears usually have names: something, some event, some person. They are the things we worry or fret over: the precious possessions we might, like Job, be divested of; the health of body that, like Job's, could disappear; the loved ones we might lose. We know the threats we fear. We see them in nightmares, muster our forces against them, plan our defenses and counterattacks.

Yet in the Gospel of Matthew, Jesus advises us not to fear the things or people who can harm the body. God attends to the needs of the sparrow, knowing every one that drops to the ground. As for us, every hair on our head is counted. We are not to worry.

The most fearless person I have known took these words of Jesus seriously. Physical discomfort, strife, censure, disappointment, foolishness in the eyes of the world, none of these could intimidate her. Even the sight of violence, whether in ugly war or mean streets, seemed not to daunt her.

She once saw a rape in progress. She did not try to hide, did not worry or fret. She simply pulled her old Volkswagen over to the sidewalk close to the sordid scene and looked at the man—his foot on the stomach of his victim. He was frozen by her light, by her sight. He insisted that she leave, escape, mind her own business. Yet she stayed with her terrible light, her fearless gaze.

After many minutes, the rapist ran. And she, with the victim, came to me and my secure community to seek help.

This woman had no fear of those who deprive the body of life. It was only later that she would fear the enemy that can destroy the soul.

After years of courageous service and stark poverty, after enduring dangers to health and safety, she came to face a deeper darkness. It was something within, a crisis of meaning, a questioning of love itself. She wrote in the journal of her last retreat:

> I felt horribly maimed inside: resigned, reduced to a very twisted, minimal sort of living, going through the motions of kindness out of habit, without hope that any kindness of mine could any longer bear real fruit. Trying to love, because there still seemed some truth in love— but mostly failing in real love for all my trying. And all around me the relentless pressure of everyone else's pain, making my own seem so trivial. . . . I come to this time in life gasping for God as if for air, needing desperately some tangible sense of God's presence with and in me. My life only makes sense if God is alive at the center of me.

It was only a little "shoot of hope lifting up amid the rubble" that she could mount against this enemy not of the body, but of the soul. "Although I am still afraid to trust the fragile reality of this experience, I think that God's love is being kindled again at the core of me. Oh, may it be so."

The last words of her journal, inspired by Archbishop Oscar Romero, spoke her desire to give that tiny bud of hope, it being all she had, to God. She took as her own the prayer of Christ who died that others might live. "Into your hands I commend my spirit." From there she began her final, most daring journey. And she was accompanied on it.

35. Letting Go the Beloved

2 Kgs. 4:8–16; Rom. 6:3–4, 8–11; Mt. 10:37–42

"Those who find their life will lose it."

In Matthew's account, Jesus tells us not to love our family members more than we love him. This text illuminates, I believe, the rather troubling formulation found in chapter 14 of Luke. Luke has it this way: "If you come to me without hating father, mother, wife, children, brothers, sisters, yes and your own life too, you cannot be my disciple." Although the word translated "hate" in Luke is closer to the original Aramaic, John L. McKenzie reminded us that Aramaic actually had no words for "love more than." Thus, the comparative softening of Matthew's "loving more than" is a fair alternative. It also provides an insight into the nature of human loves.

In scripture passages dealing with the claims human relations make upon us, at least two dangers are suggested. First, the beloved can become more important than God. Second, such love can become possessive.

If the totality of our love is exhausted by any created thing or person, then that "loved one" must become the anchor of our being, our purpose and fulfillment, our security and final hope. Sooner or later such a total object of our love becomes our idol, a false god.

But God must always be "more than" any creature of earth. If we turn a human person into a god, either that person will eventually possess us, or we will try to possess and use the fabricated god as an idol.

Psychologically this paradox makes sense, although not to the person under the spell of idolatry. If we say to another, "You're my everything; you're my meaning; I am nothing without you," then what is left of us to give that person? Why would he or she even be bothered with us, if we are nothing without them? Thus our love shatters because we are shrunk by the idolized creature without whom we would be nothing. Oddly enough, we also shrink the beloved; for there is a strategy in counterfeit love, always doomed to failure, which seeks control by investing all our attention. Parents thus suffocate the child who becomes their "everything." Love-idols are functions of a craving inadequacy; but when they fail as our "rock" or "security," we come to hate them for betraying our expectations.

The same paradox applies to the way we love ourselves. If we make ourselves the absolute goal of our seeking, we bring ruin upon ourselves. Only when we die to such narcissistic illusions can we be fulfilled. Only when we take up the cross of true love—"laying down our lives," sharing ourselves freely with our family and friends, not demanding that they be our gods or we be theirs—do we find ourselves.

If neither I nor you are God, but only God is God, then we may love each other freely, nonpossessively, and without jealousy. There is no question of domination or control. Then we know the greatest gift God has given us, the capacity to bestow our lives freely in covenants and promises to our dear ones, who even in eternity are loved in God.

"Whoever welcomes you, welcomes me and the one who sent me," Jesus said. In this life and the next, when we so welcome each other, we truly love the God who dwells in us and yet is not reduced to us.

36. Setting Free the Flesh

Zech. 9:9–10; Rom. 8:9–13; Mt. 11:25–30

"My yoke is easy, my burden light."

Paul is famous for his suspicions about the body. His own words make him suspect. "If you live according to the flesh, you will die; but if by the spirit you put to death the evil deeds of the body, you will live." Such texts have opened Paul to the charge that he is anti-body, even Manichaean, in his theology.

We know, however, that Paul's view is far more nuanced than might first be suspected. The word *sarx*, "flesh," does not indicate the same reality as *soma*, "body," the latter word being far more integrative and unifying than the former. But the human body or *soma* can be jailed in the prison of mere flesh if it is without the liberty of spirit and soul.

Mere flesh, *sarx*, the debased, sin-ruled body, is earth-bound human existence left to itself. Flesh, in this sense, is dominated by the organic drives for self-maintenance and enhancement, even at the expense of others, until the force of death holds sway. The rigid rule of these drives makes any thought of spirit, freedom, or love impossible. That is why, in the Letter to the Galatians, chapter 5, Paul describes the law of the flesh as wild sexual irresponsibility, slavery, and violent jealousy.

How Freudian this sounds. Freud, considered passé in some psychiatric circles but the rage in cultural studies, articulated most fully the logic of flesh, or *sarx*. In *The Future of an Illusion,* a critique of religious faith, he deemed that our primordial organic desires are incest, cannibalism, and killing. Even those who, under civilization's hard constraint, shrink from incest or murder, "do not deny themselves the satisfaction of avarice, their aggressive urges or sexual lusts, and do not hesitate to injure others by lies, fraud, and calumny, so long as they can remain unpunished for it."

This sounds like the world of *sarx* in Romans and Galatians. Freud has nothing on Paul when it comes to unmasking the raw and deadly face of flesh closed in upon itself. Without civic prohibitions, we would "take any one as a sexual object, kill any rival or anyone else who stands in the way, and carry off any of the other's belongings." Freud proposed that science, rather than religion, might save us from ourselves. The voice of intellect, he said, would be heard and, he hoped, obeyed.

Both in his own thought and in subsequent years, however, it would prove to be the other way around. The tiresome labor of flesh-bound mind is powerless to escape the yoke of blind lust, violence, and avarice. Science, like the flesh that makes it, merely delays the heavy burdensome end of life's labor. "For the aim of all life is death."

Paul the psychologist understood this. The life he knew, however, transcended the world of mere flesh. The body inspirited could become a temple of eternal promise. It could sing of love, play in joy, console with gentle compassion, touch with kindness—all those gifts of the Spirit that make the human body revelatory of God. Unlike Freud's flesh, in turmoil, condemned to labor and death, Paul's is transcended by the spirit of Jesus, who invites us:

> Come to me, all you who are weary and find life burdensome, and I will refresh you. Take my yoke upon your shoulders and learn from me, for I am gentle and humble of heart. Your souls will find rest, for my yoke is easy and my burden is light.

37. The Problem of Evil

Is. 55:10–11; Rom. 8:18–23; Mt. 13:1–23

"All creation groans."

Creation has its cost. To be creature, not creator, is to be incomplete, unfinished. Created being is radically insufficient to cause and sustain itself. Thus God, in willing that there be non-god, had to will that there be frailty and incompleteness. Such is the price of creaturehood.

And yet, even though creation is not God, it is still precious in its unfinished and dependent state. Think of the human hand, so delicate in its strength, so supple and alert, so sensitive and expressive. Yet it can be smashed in a moment, cut off, wounded. Is it better off not to exist? Or is the hand, despite its frailty, glorious? Is its frailty its glory?

An infant's giggle, a child's untrammeled laughter—these disarm and delight. Yet the same enchanted voice can sound doom: utter rage and fear, alarm at the terrors of the night and the demons of the playground. Would it have been better to make us all unfeeling, unlaughing, unhurtable?

We are inherently deficient and wanting, inescapably vulnerable. Such is the pain of the earth. Yet the sufferings of time, Paul writes, are nothing compared to the glory revealed in us. There is futility in our being only if our being is all there is. The flower fades and droops. The once young body one day sags and then lingers long. Flesh hardens first, then melts away, corruptible, slave to space and time. And yet we glory in it, and rightly so. God does as well. This paltry flesh, like all creation groaning, longs for finish, completion, and rest. Such is the glorious agony of our condition.

We, like the earth that gives birth to us, are subject to the great inexorable laws of rise and decay. We are fundamentally good, we are growing things; and yet because we grow, we lack. The name for this mystery beneath the formation of mountain ridges and spinal cords is physical evil, deficiency, the parasite of an unfinished universe that is good.

But the appearance of human life raised the stakes: the joys and the catastrophes. For into this world were cast creatures not only unfinished in their being, but in their nature. Men and women were gifted not just with life, but with life aware of itself, endowed with the freedom to affirm or reject the limited good that they were.

Mountains show might, and seas roar, but humans utter, "Yes." They might also say, "No." And it was that yes or no that made us worth God's final risk. In addition to the great play of organic development, there would be the drama of free choice. From such a creation would come not only the glories of love, but the catastrophes of moral evil.

Some of us would not understand at all. On the paths of life, unrooted, our freedom is pecked at by passing birds. For others, the freedom dries and withers. Still others choke their choice in fear and worldly anxiety. But then, others take it all in. They embrace the limit of life, the gift of being good but not God. They cherish the gift of dependence as creatures. And they bear fruit a thousand times more splendid than the bounty of trees.

> Just as from the heavens the rain and snow come down
> and do not return there till they have watered the earth,
> so shall my word be that goes forth from my mouth. It
> shall not return to me void, but shall do my will,
> achieving the end for which I sent it.

38. In Our Weakness

Wis. 12:13, 16–19; Rom. 8:26–27; Mt. 13:24–43

"The kingdom of heaven is like . . . "

We are so small, we humans. The odds against any one of us existing are so stupendous the numbers dwarf us. A hundred million of our father's sperm—sifted down to a few dozen that reached the neighborhood of one particular ovum at one fleeting moment—were other possible candidates for life, not us. In most cases, one seed joins one egg in the start of you or me. Multiply this event by days and months and years of fertility, other possible spouses and lost ancestors, and the unlikelihood of our being conceived is greater than our chances to win the super-lottery every day of a lifetime. Yet, here we are, in a solar system that is a speck in a field of stars. Creation is like that, a great lotto of life, a sea of rushing graces and missed chances.

In all the happenstance of history and space, the good lasts, the gospel tells us. It is worth the vast expenditure of matter and energy to gain the good. It is worth all the misfortune to reap the benefit. Fruit grows amid the weeds. Life and waste walk hand in hand. Gain and loss are partners. But the loss, the waste, is endured for the sake of the yield.

What is more, the fruit starts so small. Like one act of love, one time of kindness, one moment of courage, growth is imperceptible in the seeding. The mustard seed, once so tiny, becomes a great shrub, the home to wayfaring birds of passage. So it is in Jesus' other analogy for the reign of God: a bit of yeast permeates and quickens the batch of flour.

The use of parables, a tradition rooted in wisdom and rabbinical literature, is a hallmark of Jesus' teaching. No doubt the particular images of mustard seed and leaven struck home not only to his hearers, but also to the early Christian community, quite conscious of the worldly insignificance of Jesus and its own smallness in contrast to Judaism and the Roman Empire. They believed the reign of God would come, just as surely as the harvest, despite obstacles and setbacks.

But there is a psychological dimension to these parables that far transcends the particularities of history and circumstance.

We are so afraid of our smallness. On the scale of matter, big is better. What is large is impressive. The grand is good. The small seems weak and vulnerable. But thinking so, we fail to see the wisdom of life, the promise of smallness, the world not of mere matter, but of spirit.

Have we not all felt the grace that rises from the least? The early free smile of a child? The first kiss? The initial act of kindness? The fragile promise made with full heart? Each of us, so inconsequential in history's chamber, so lost in vast spaces measured by light years, bears a power not quantified by weight and measure. The human heart, small and frail by cosmic standards, rises to heights out of its very frailty when it loves, hopes, and believes. This is what the reign of God is all about. And it is in our hearts that God's Spirit moves.

That tiny instant wherein we started bears fruit, not only in a lifetime that itself is small, but in love that inhabits a realm beyond the reign of size and number.

39. The Higher Wisdom

1 Kgs. 3:5–12; Rom. 8:29–30; Mt. 13:44–52

"A heart, wise and understanding."

Some prominent sages have written that the root desires of human existence are the pride of power, the accumulation of money, and the experience of pleasure. Thinkers like Hobbes, Ayn Rand, Machiavelli, and the Marquis de Sade have built great ideologies on one of the competing life-goals of sex, power, and money. This opinion is not limited to ivory tower theoreticians; it's expressed in the language of ordinary people when they appeal to the "real" motives lurking behind all human actions: "Looking out for Number One," "We're all out for a buck," "Everybody's on the make."

The billions spent on advertising presume, quite successfully, that the foundations of all value and meaning are things, privilege, and self-indulgence. A computer ad announces that you can "Satisfy Your Lust for Power and Money," in a new reconstruction of the ancient religious vows. Reformulations of Descartes's "Cogito ergo sum," appear as "I want, therefore I am," "I shop, therefore I am," "I win, therefore I am." Yamaha says, "Beat thy neighbor." Nike Corporation has even mounted an entire advertising campaign on the celebration of pleasure: "We are all basically hedonists. That's what makes us human. And we all want, all we've ever wanted is to have a good time. If it feels good, then just do it."

It was not a marketing huckster, but Solomon's God who offered in a dream, "Ask something of me and I will give it to you." As it turned out, it was not a good time that Solomon sought. While most people might ask for bliss or some prized object identified with fulfillment—an advertiser's dream, to be sure—Solomon requested wisdom. Perhaps that is why God seems a bit amazed (if God can be amazed) by the fact that Solomon's deepest desire is not for a long life or riches or success over enemies, but for a heart that can distinguish right from wrong. Solomon, famous for his riches, found his real treasure in a wise and understanding heart. It was in knowing right from wrong that he found joy.

What is our treasure that, once found, is worth all we can sell or trade? What is the pearl of great price for which we would sacrifice everything? This is what the gospel's reign of God is about: our hearts' desire, our deepest existential longing.

Some seek pleasures in every variation imaginable. They fall away sated but restless. Some build shrines to the ego's power. They die alone, unloved, and uncaring. Others collect their things to die, like the movies' Citizen Kane, empty of substance.

Solomon dreamed long ago that a higher wisdom and deeper joy might be found. It would not be grasped in the accumulation of things, the collection of earthly delights, or dominance over others, even though these would be given to him in good time. His deepest desire was to know a good that was fully worth loving. His highest hope was to know what was right and to be able to do it. God saw this higher wisdom in him, this pearl of great price, and Solomon's wish was granted.

For the treasures of his heart, not his mines, Solomon is rightly remembered.

40. The Higher Love

Is. 55:1–3; Rom. 8:35–39; Mt. 14:13–21

"Nothing can separate us from the love of God."

For the longest time I misread the meaning of Paul's passage on the love of Christ. It was the "of" that threw me. I took it to mean our love of God, not God's love of us. Thus, trial or persecution or threats should not shake our love. No creature should come between us and our love for God, no power should overcome us. Love, in this reading, was a task to do, an achievement to be strived for. Our faith was a noble task of steadfast love on *our* part.

It is quite clear, however, that Paul is saying something else: nothing in existence can ever separate us from the love that God, revealed in Jesus, has for us. Not only does the first interpretation miss the boat by focusing on our attitudes and desires; it fosters one of the most persistent mistakes about our faith. Christian faith is not primarily about something we do for God. It is about what God does for and in us. It is not so much an account of human aspiration as it is a revelation of divine desire.

The covenant that Isaiah promised to David's progeny could not be bought or earned. It was there for the taking, like water for the thirsty to drink. It was the gift of food that need not be purchased, wine and milk without cost. All we need do is accept the offer.

This could be troubling. Does it mean that we don't have to work at all? Is our faith effortless? Are our actions, good or sinful, inconsequential in the eyes of God?

It certainly seems not. After all, the dragnet parable about the reign of God from this week's longer gospel reading suggests that we humans perform both good and evil acts. More troubling still, it seems that at the end of the world there will be a host of angels who will separate the wicked from the just and cast the wicked into a fire, where they will grind their teeth. That statement sounds as though we actually can be separated from the love of God. It also sounds scary.

What's going on here? Is it possible that the refusal of the gift, the rejection of God's love, can separate us? Is faith in the promise, hope in the covenant, acceptance of the love, the work we must do, the only effort we must make to avoid damnation? Of that I'm not sure; it raises the awesome question whether anyone is eternally lost.

But I do believe the words of the psalmist suggest an answer: "The Lord is gracious and merciful, slow to anger and of great kindness. The Lord is good to all and compassionate toward all his works. The Lord is just in all his ways and holy in all his deeds. The Lord is near to all who call upon him, to all who call upon him in truth."

Jesus, his heart moved by compassion, cured the sick. More tellingly, when his disciples wanted to dismiss the pressing crowd to search for food, he told his followers to offer their own food freely. Five loaves and two fish fed thousands, the fragments filling twelve bushels. Maybe there is such a thing as a free lunch.

Somewhere in the mystery of God is an unlimited bounty, whether it makes sense to us or not. This God we meet in Jesus just does not work according to our ways. It may not make for good business, it may even be bad law, but whatever else it is, it seems to be God's way of loving.

41. God in the Quiet and the Chaos

1 Kgs. 19:9–13; Rom. 9:1–5; Mt. 14:22–33

"They cried out in fear."

Elijah, having been promised that he would find the Lord on the mountain, left the shelter of his cave. Sure enough, God showed up, but not in mighty gales or crashing rocks. The Lord was not even encountered in the earthquake or the fiery extravaganza. It was a tiny whispering voice that made Elijah cover his face in the presence of the Most High. Elijah was called in the quiet.

Peter and his companions, tossed about by waves and wind, saw the Lord as a ghost upon the water and were terrified. The voice over the tumult said: "Get hold of yourselves! It is I! Do not be afraid!" Peter heard the call to cross the raging waters. But daunted by the strength of the wind and his own frailty, he began to sink in fear. Even so, despite his going under, Peter was called to faith in the midst of turmoil.

Some of us imagine that God is found only in the gentle whisper, the nook of isolation, the mountain of retreat and quiet. And indeed the call is often heard there, far from the noise and distraction, not in turbulence but in serenity.

But that should not lead us to believe that the storms of life signal godforsakenness. Too easily suspecting that terrors are graceless, we ignore the strongest calls made in days of strife and struggle. Rather than think our fears indicate a loss of moorings, we should imagine them as opportunities for deeper anchor.

Fears rise as invitations to greater trust, if we only face them and move through them. Once back in the boat, the storm past, we are able to say with a faith hitherto unfelt, "Beyond doubt you are the Son of God."

Fear most often assails us, it seems to me, when we are in danger of losing something or someone we cling to. It is understandable that we would worry about the possibility of losing something, someone, some strength in ourselves so reliable and so dear. But the threat of loss is the call across troubled waters.

The sinking feeling may be nothing other than the recognition of our inability to walk the waters on our own. Going under despite our efforts, we finally turn our faces up more honestly, more in faith, to the one who carries us. Ebbing powers and promise do not signal the end. They remind us that it is only in God that we are strong. Fright does not necessarily mean cowardice; it also invites the admission that we are wondrously dependent.

Storms are omens of deliverance as well as of disaster. If we break through to freedom in the following calm, we discover a faith in God so newly grounded that we need never again fear losing the cherished creatures we love. A radical faith, the daughter of dark times, finds the sun wherein all the loves we have had are illumined in the love that is light.

If fear is the last word in our love, we will communicate only fear to those we cherish. Such fear is a futile strain, as if we could walk, by our puny skills, on water. But fear faced and released in faith allows us to love the beloved more freely and the giver of the gift more authentically.

Twentieth Sunday in Ordinary Time

42. All Equal, Each Unique

Is. 56:6–7; Rom. 11:13–15, 29–32; Mt. 15:21–28

"Woman, you have great faith."

That ancient problem of the one and the many has taken a million shapes. It is seen in the battle of change with continuity, the clash of novelty with permanence, the claims of individuality versus universality.

The conflict also appears in passages of scripture that contrast the particularities of Judaism or Christianity with the universality of God. Isaiah announced a God whose salvation and justice would be open to aliens. "For my house shall be called a house of prayer for all peoples." Thus, the psalmist wrote that all nations would come to praise God. St. Paul, in his reconciling claims of Jew and Gentile, reminded the Romans that a more universal truth of God's mercy is revealed in the failures of both.

Even the accounts of Jesus' meetings with Gentiles balance the claims of inclusion and exclusion. He seems rather harsh to the Canaanite woman who seeks healing for her demon-possessed daughter. At first Jesus does not even respond, and his disciples nag him to dismiss her because of her stubborn shouts. When Jesus remarks that his mission is only to the lost sheep of Israel, the woman presses her point, not only begging more insistently for help, but rebutting his rejection. "Even the dogs eat the leavings that fall from their master's tables."

Although the issue of tribal and religious inclusion might be discussed here, especially in light of Isaiah's promise of univer-salism and Paul's appeal to Gentile and Jew, what might be more key about this story is the revelation of that common trait of all men and women which engages the healing power of Jesus.

It is the heart, the plea, the persistent hope. "Woman, you have great faith. Your wish will come to pass." And her daughter is healed.

The Canaanite woman embodies the constant and universal quality that every human heart—Jew or Gentile, woman or man, slave or free—possesses. It was her and our own willing-ness to call out in faith. This power, slumbering in us all from the moment of our beginnings in our mothers' wombs, whether ever actualized or not, is what each of us uniquely possesses and yet has in common with all the rest of us. From the time of Sarah and Abraham to Mary's yes and Joseph's word of trust, from Romans to rabbis, Africans to Indians, it is the endowment of our personhood that unites us all in our humanity. It is also what makes every one of us singularly strategic in playing our particular life drama.

Human persons are endowed with the capacity to take possession of their lives and offer their lives in faith. This is what makes every man and woman wholly equal before the world and God.

Yet the universal blessing of our humanity is found only in individuals. Each of us must act out the drama of a single life alone. There is no understudy, no replacement in these matters. Our common gift is displayed in singular and particular beauty. Thus, the paradox of the one and the many is that the very gift that makes us all most alike makes each of us altogether unique.

43. Rock of Ages

Is. 22:15,19–23; Rom. 11:33–36; Mt. 16:13–20

"Who could know the mind of God?"

"What's happened to the church? The last council seems to be the work of the devil." The words still stay with me, although I heard them from an older priest many years ago.

He died not long after, and I often wonder what he would think if he were still alive. The apparently serene and steady church he once knew, that ark of sure safety, has been sailing troubled waters, to say the least.

Elders question whether our young know enough dogma or tradition to pass anything on to their future children. Nagging doubts stimulate questions: does the language of holiness and transcendence, of sin and forgiveness, of objective right and wrong, of the sacred and eternal even make sense to most Catholics?

Divisions are so stark and sharp, one invites complete perplexity by daring to read conservative and liberal Catholic publications in the same sitting. The demons of one pose as angels for the other. Actions judged sinful by some Catholics are called virtuous by others. The papacy of Pope John Paul II inspires pride, hope, and trust for some, bitter disappointment—even anger—in others. Vocations to the priesthood and to the once-thriving religious congregations dwindle, despite the stronger showing among communities that are more conservative or "orthodox."

If we even halfway agree with this account, what might we think of Christ's words to Peter? "You are Rock, and on this rock I will build my church, and the jaws of death shall not prevail against it." This text, understood both in terms of papal primacy and the church's durability, surely challenges the faith of the contemporary Catholic.

But when has it not been so? What kind of "rock" was Peter when only moments after his great profession, "You are the Messiah, the Son of the living God," Jesus would say, "Get behind me, you have the thoughts of Satan"? That was only the beginning of Peter's reign, through braggadocio, denials, betrayals, reconciliations, victories, later struggles with Paul, and disappointments with his people.

As for Peter's ark, that church, our church, how often it neared disaster: in the shadow of imperial armies, under threats of martyrdom and flame, in the depths of dark ages, infidelities of monks, scandals of popes, in the great wounds of schism, the slaughter of religious wars, the unraveling of the priesthood, the selling of bishoprics, the seductions of fascism, Communism, and capitalism.

Yet doom was not our destiny. Through all of history's storms, despite infidelities, diminishments, and failure, the church has carried in its womb, to be born over and over again in scripture and the Eucharist, the Christ who asks of us, whether pope or peasant, "Who do you say I am?" And by its children, from Borgia palaces to the huts of Connemara, in the convents of Lisieux and in the slave ships of Cartagena's harsh harbors, on Korea's crosses or Colorado's mountain hermitages, the answer which made Peter a rock and the church an ark was given: "You are the Messiah, the Son of the living God."

St. Paul plumbed the mystery. "How deep are the riches and the wisdom and the knowledge of God. How inscrutable his judgments, how unsearchable his ways."

44. Not Conforming to the Age

Jer. 20:7–9; Rom. 12:1–2; Mt. 16:21–27

"You are not judging by God's standards."

Our desire for equilibrium fools us. Smooth sailing and steady stability, we suppose, should be the by-products of faith. That's why we often secretly hope to experience a baptism in the Spirit to end all baptisms or a mighty conversion that solves everything once and for all. But like Jeremiah, we soon enough find out that the calling of God is not the beginning of tranquillity.

"You duped me, O Lord, and I let myself be duped; you were too strong for me, and you triumphed." Jeremiah would live to be mocked, laughed at, derided. Eventually, he told God he'd had enough. To no avail. "It is like a fire burning in my heart, imprisoned in my bones; I grow weary holding it in, I cannot endure it." The gift of prophecy required a life of resistance.

So it is with discipleship according to Paul. "Do not conform yourselves to this age, but be transformed by the renewal of your mind, so that you may judge what is God's will."

Even Peter had a hard time accepting the cost of discipleship. Within moments of his confirmation as leader, he is protesting the struggle, the pain, the failure, and the rejection that Jesus foretells. "May you be spared, Master. God forbid that any such thing ever happen to you." But Jesus rebukes Peter: "Get out of my sight, you satan! You are trying to make me trip and fall. You are not judging by God's standards, but by human ones."

Following Christ costs the follower. What must be paid is a willingness to let go of our hunger for security, approval, and comfort; to take up our own cross of love and give ourselves away, to abandon our images of success and schemes of self-indulgence.

The lure of holiness, as Jeremiah found out to his discomfort, provides no warm blanket. Love's love is no crutch, as some critics of religion have imagined. No, it is a harrowing experience, something like a death. Only radical insecurity remains when we entrust all to God, especially our disappointments and failure.

We live in an age when, by all cultural accounts, our faith is foolish. Our ritual is weirdly transcendent. Our vows appear to be unkeepable promises, our sacraments quaint. The practices we aspire to are held in high suspicion. It is impossible, we are told, for people to be chaste. It is idiotic not to choose what pleases or fulfills us. This cultural skepticism is so deep in our own bones that we, like Peter, balk before the truth Christ proposes. How often do our church, our preaching, our practice, merely ape the culture's love of money, power, and privilege? The way of faith reaches too high; its paths are too arduous.

Yet in daunting times, let us recall Peter, who himself endured the same. Peter does "get behind" Jesus but does not give up because of his failure. He follows to Jerusalem, even though he fears. He follows to Gethsemane, even though he sleeps there. He follows to the Passion, even though he hides. He waits for Christ in the upper room, even though he is shamed by his betrayals.

May the church Peter once led, despite all its harrowing trials, have faith to do the same.

45. Challenge in Community

Ez. 33:7–9; Rom. 13:8–10; Mt. 18:15–20

"Go, and point out the fault."

As if particularly sensitive to the demands of Christian community life, the readings from the Lectionary's Cycle A this
month provide contrasting sets of virtues and vices that foster
and destroy relationships. Willingness to communicate and
forgive enhances a common life of faith. Jealousy and envy, as
we will see in subsequent weeks, rip communities apart.

Community life, whether in a family, intentional group-
ings, religious congregations, or the church itself, is the great
testing ground of faith. St. Teresa of Avila thought that relationships in community were often a greater indication of
one's relationship to God than the heights of mystical prayer.
An activist like Dorothy Day was wise enough to see that
injustice and exploitation were as present in small service
communities as in political empires. And Jean Vanier, as
committed to marginal people as anyone might be, has often
observed that it takes greater charity and humility to get along
with a co-laborer than with a handicapped stranger.

Paul reminds his Roman audience that love, tested in im-
mediate relationship with our neighbor, is the fulfillment of all
laws. Even dramatic sins of adultery, murder, and stealing are
variations of the more domestic betrayals of deception, manip-
ulation, and egotism. In each case it is a lack of love, a
harming of the neighbor, that occurs. This is why our one
duty, our sole "debt," is to love one another.

Today's gospel provides a practical scenario on community relations: "If your brother should commit some wrong
against you, go and point out his fault, but keep it between

the two of you. . . . If he does not listen, summon another, so that every case may stand on the word of two or three witnesses." Only after these careful encounters is the conflict to be referred to the entire church. Then, if recalcitrance persists, there is separation.

Sounds simple enough. The problem is, it depends upon behaviors that do not come easily. We don't often enjoy directly confronting another person, especially someone with whom we are having difficulties. Some families will go years before addressing a problem. Grudges or resentments within a community more often die with those who hold them rather than come to resolution in quiet conversation. Misdeeds of friends or relatives are usually discussed with anyone but the accused.

Encountering the truth with another person daunts us because it makes us face another being who cannot be reduced to our own desires or projections. We may try to make others a function of our egos, but it fails. Rather than enter the struggle, we ignore it.

If, however, we seriously love another person as an "other," and not a mere instrument of our wills, we experience the kind of self-transcendence that is required in our relationship to God.

Is it any wonder, then, that what we bind and loose on earth is somehow bound and loosed eternally? Our human relationships mirror our relationship with God. Whenever we encounter each other—not only in prayer—Jesus is in our midst.

46. Forgiveness in Community

Sir. 27:30–28:7; Rom. 14:7–9; Mt. 18:21–35

"Slow to anger, rich in compassion."

This gospel is a troubling tale. Jesus tells a parable of a king settling accounts with a debtor who begs for patience. Out of pity, the king writes off the debt. But when that same official throttles a servant who pleads for similar patience, the king, hearing of the incident, renounces the one he had forgiven and has him tortured "until he paid" (however that might be done). "My Father," Jesus concludes, "will treat you the same way."

What happened to "seventy times seven times"? The king's sentencing of the first debtor to torture doesn't seem so very forgiving—especially after only one failing.

The key is that the failing is radical unforgiveness. It's as if the refusal to forgive, by its very nature, locks us into a torturous circle. So tightly closed against pardoning the other, we have sealed ourselves off from the very experience of pardon.

It is hard to believe that God could forgive endlessly. We surely would not. Forgive again and again and again? We think that if we forgive too easily, people—our children, our spouses, our friends, our enemies—will walk all over us. We offer ourselves more "realistic" counsel. "I'll forgive, maybe once, or if they forgive me first, or if there is some promise of change, or if they don't do it again, or if they acknowledge their sin."

But such a tactic leads to a tortured soul. The weight of unforgiven hurt bends and burdens us. We carry grudges like clinkers, burnt up and cold.

The great tragedy is that if we wish to exempt ourselves from the law of Jesus, the law of love and forgiveness; if we establish for ourselves a new reality; if vengeance and retribution are what we embrace as most true and reliable, then that is what we are left with. Hell is not so much the punishment of God as it is the result that our punishment of each other demands.

In the church, in our families, in our hearts, we have all experienced the logic of unforgiveness. Even at the age of five, a child might be heard to mutter, "I'll never talk to them again." If the judgment hardens, it is only the heart of the judger that grows cold. The words, "I will never forgive you," can shut tight the heart of the one who utters them, definitively deadened and alone.

It is true, as the psalmist said, that "the Lord is kind and merciful, slow to anger and rich in compassion." But in our refusal to accept the reality of Jesus, we enthrone the reality of resentment as the law of life. There is an unyielding recalcitrance about unforgiveness. It is a rejection of love. We refuse to give it; we make it impossible to receive it.

When the Lord answers Peter's question, how often we should forgive, he says, "not seven times but seventy times seven times." Jesus is not recommending a mathematics of reconciliation. He is using the extreme numbers to suggest the unbridgeable chasm between a forgiving and an unforgiving universe. His parable may be less about the retribution of God than it is about a state of soul so hardened that even a kind and compassionate God could not soften it.

47. Envious Comparisons

Is. 55:1–9; Phil. 1:20–24, 27; Mt. 20:1–16

"Are you envious because I am generous?"

It continues to amaze me that some people think God is a projection of humanity's wish. That may be true of idols or false gods, but it just doesn't work with the God of Moses and the prophets, the God made flesh in Jesus. This God doesn't act or behave as we would. It is not just that God is more merciful than we might be, or more forgiving; God seems not even to think the way we do. As Isaiah reminds us, "As high as the heavens are above the earth, so high are my ways above your ways and my thoughts above your thoughts."

Of course, God starts from a different place. Having all that is required, God's actions do not spring from need, unless it be the need to give. The whole point of God's love is in giving something to the other. We needy creatures, however, act most basically out of insufficiency. It is understandable that we perceive all love in terms of fulfilling our lack. The other, whether God, human, animal, or thing, stands before us to serve our needs.

What is more, other beings stand as competitors. They, too, need. They want the same things we want. And their gain seems our loss. Not for nothing did Jean Paul Sartre, in one of his more rancorous moments, claim that hell was other people.

W. H. Auden wrote:

> For the error bred in the bone
> Of each woman and each man
> Craves what it cannot have:

Not universal love,
But to be loved alone.

As Abel was a threat to Cain, so it has ever been.

No one needs to teach us to compete for love. A child, little more than a year old, will scream at the telephone's intrusion on a mother's attention. At the age of two, the threat of the other becomes so strong that some toddlers will literally hold and turn the face of the parent to grab back the gaze momentarily given to someone else. By three, some children seem most interested in toys when someone else is in the room who might dare to touch them.

"Who do you love best?" These are the words of a child who fears losing something when there are other children in the family. "I love all of you equally," is never a satisfying answer. When the rest are out of the room, the question persists: "Now you can tell me; who do you really love best?"

"Am I your best friend?" Teenagers are not the only ones who harbor the hope to be number one, to be the one and only. Sharing the love of a special friend with someone else is rarely an occasion for toasts. It is rather like the loss of a nonrenewable natural resource. A new friend, a third member to the group, is like an invading army. And when we ourselves were unwelcome newcomers to a dyad, how often have we felt like a useless "third wheel"?

"Why am I not enough for you?" One hears the refrain from adults. A spouse says to the beloved: "Why do you need to go out with your friends? Why do you spend so much time doing things I don't care for? Am I not enough?" And I have heard the answer to the crestfallen questioner: "No, you are not enough. I love you and you're my 'one and only' and you're good to be with. But you are not everything." Such is the error "bred in the bone."

In our more honest and alert moments, Christ's parable of the estate owner and the hired hands might well distress us. Some hard-working and enterprising souls start laboring in the

vineyard at dawn. Subsequent groups, no doubt less resource-
ful, arrive at noon, mid-afternoon, and late afternoon and are
put to work by the landowner. Finally, at the moment of pay-
off, those hired late receive a full day's pay—and get paid first.

Those who started working at the break of day are not
pleased with such a sweet deal: "This last group did only an
hour's work, but you have put them on the same basis as us,
who have worked a full day in the scorching heat." But the
landowner, claiming that no injustice was done or agreement
broken, does not accept their complaint. "I am free to do as I
please with my money, am I not? Or are you envious because I
am generous?"

Now, just judge that I am, and aspiring lawyer that I have
been since infancy, I think the complainers had a point. The
arrangement just isn't fair. (How many times have we spoken
or heard this refrain?) Surely the full-day workers did more to
win the rewards of payment and approval. Surely they should
have some compensation to match their efforts and achievement. By any just comparison or calculus of effort, they
deserve more.

But more of what? More love? More happiness? How could
there be more of that, unless love and happiness were themselves in some way unsatisfying to us? This matter of grace,
this life of the kingdom, is not a calculus of rationality. It is a
bountiful gratuity.

St. Paul seems to have felt this mystery of abundance. Even
the greatest goods of life no longer hold him in thrall. He loves
them, true. But it is a love that has ceased to grasp or compare.
It is finally a love that gives, that says "yes" rather than, "You
must be mine and mine alone."

48. Love's Labor

Ez. 18:25–28; Phil. 2:1–11; Mt. 21:28–32

"Not something to be grasped at."

In *The Brothers Karamazov,* Dostoevsky tells the tale of Madam Holakov's confession to the monk Zossima. The old woman, doubting her destiny in the face of death, presumes her crisis is of faith. Father Zossima, however, sees the problem as one of love.

When he advises Holakov to labor at loving her neighbors as a way to dispel her worries, she realizes he has struck a nerve. There is no doubt, she thinks, that she loves humanity; but the actual doing of it, the living of it, gives her pause. The old priest, concurring with her, recounts the story of a disillusioned doctor who had great dreams of universal love but bitter disappointments in dealing with the real thing. "I love humanity," he said, "but the more I love humanity in general, the less I love people in particular." While his dreams portray visions of saving humankind, in his daily life the good doctor can't stand the people around him. "I am incapable of living in the same room with anyone for two days together. . . . As soon as anyone is near me, his personality disturbs me and restricts my freedom." The slightest irritation rattles the poor man's nerves. He bristles at the way someone talks, sneers at the way someone walks or wheezes, and can barely tolerate the manner of someone's dress or bearing. "In twenty-four hours I begin to hate the best of men. . . . I become hostile to people the moment they come close to me."

For most of us, God is not the problem. The problem is those humans that God created, especially the creeps who don't deserve to exist, or at least those who bother us. When people draw near, they bring trouble. Anyone close to us sooner or later restricts our precious freedom.

St. Paul had a great sense of this paradox: the best indication of our highest reach for God is the person within arm's reach. That is why relationship in community or family is so inextricably woven into our relationship with God. It is not just that the two "great commandments"—wholeheartedly loving God and loving our neighbors as ourselves—are similar. It's that our very relationships to each other embody our relationship to God.

Paul's Letter to the Philippians is well known for its great hymn to Christ Jesus, "who, though he was in the form of God, did not regard equality with God as something to be exploited, but emptied himself, taking the form of a servant, being born in human likeness." It was in Jesus' serving, in his "emptying" of himself, even his acceptance of death on the cross, that he found fullness and the everlasting praise of history.

But this exalted hymn is the application of a way of life that Paul has recommended in our relationships to each other. The hymn exemplifies the "mind" of Christ that we must "put on" when we face each other. We will find joy and consolation only when we die to ourselves: an unwelcome prospect. The reason why people avoid parenting (not just making babies) is the cost. The reason we avoid community life is the challenge it makes to our narcissism. In authentic relationship, the love we dream about is tested and purified by the actualities of "this particular person at this particular time."

The problem of Dostoevsky's frightened old lady and cynical doctor is that they both want love, but not its cost. They know they are in trouble, but they do not have the will to labor at the solution. For love is more than logic, proofs, or rationality. It is a risk of the ego, an emptying of the self, a desire to serve rather than to be served. This risk is the crux of the Christian belief in the mystery of love: first, that God would love us; second, that we, graced by such bounty, might generously love others.

St. Paul is inescapably direct: "In the name of the encouragement you owe me in Christ, in the name of the solace that love can give, of fellowship in spirit, compassion, and pity, I beg you, make my joy complete by your unanimity, possessing the one love, united in spirit and ideals. Never act out of rivalries or conceit; rather let all parties think humbly of others as superior to themselves, each of you looking to others' interests rather than his own. Your attitude must be Christ's."

But that is the very attitude we resist. We live on rivalry, we cherish our conceits. Our rarest concern is the other's good—unless it is hard won through arduous relationships of covenant and trust.

In the story Jesus told to the chief priests and elders, one son mouths the words but does not act; the other son resists at first but eventually labors in the vineyard. The second child actually does God's will. Words are not enough. That is why converted tax collectors and prostitutes enter the kingdom before those who merely talk of righteousness.

We jabber of love. But the living of it requires a great winnowing of our lives, a shaking down of our pretense. Love in dreams, Dostoevsky wrote, is easy; but the reality of it is a dreadful assault—not on our deepest longings, but on those tawdry delusions that pose as solutions to them.

49. The Vineyard Church

Is. 5:1–7; Phil. 4:6–9; Mt. 21:33–43

"He looked for justice, but hark, the outcry!"

We delude ourselves dangerously if we think our major task in reading scripture is to examine the historical period in which it was written. Admittedly, such study is a valuable tool for critical distance from and understanding of revelation's context.

But if the word of God lives for us, it must be spoken now. It must be received now. Paul's charge to the Philippians is that they live what they have learned and accepted. Living the word, more than the study of it, yields "God's own peace beyond all understanding."

If we are concerned only with knowing the historical context of Isaiah's vineyard story, we may find out something about the people of Judah and their infidelities, but we will miss what the prophet has to say to us. And if prophets have nothing to say to us, why bother listening to them at all?

What if our contemporary church is seen as the new House of Israel, God's cherished vineyard? What if we are that land, carefully cleared of stones, now filled with vines delicately planted? Then Isaiah's words might shake us. "He looked for judgment, but saw bloodshed! He looked for justice, but heard cries." Despite everything that was done for this vineyard, despite all that was given, there was no true yield. So the owner gave the verdict: it shall all be torn down, eroded, and trampled, overgrown with briars and thorns. Are these words addressed to our church?

There is a temptation to make our holy books, even our privileged "New" Testament readings, into a collection of quaint bygone accounts, comfortably shelved in a mausoleum. Now and then, we prod the dead text, safely kept at arm's length, with some thin academic stick that protects us from what we poke.

When Jesus looks at scripture, it's a different story. He recalls Isaiah's parable of the vineyard, but only to engage it for his own time and people. The leaders of his age were rejecting him, son of the vineyard's Lord, just as they rejected the delegations of prophets before him. What is worse, they reject him as the Son of God, even kill him, in the false hope that they will then get the inheritance for themselves.

When the church applies this gospel story merely to Jesus' context, two things happen. A crude conclusion is drawn that the chief priests and elders (and even the Jewish people, as the story was later diabolically interpreted) were the source of Christ's rejection. More foolish yet, we Christians presume that we ourselves do not reject Christ in our own lives.

At our safe distance, we can shake our heads. See the results of their rejection of Jesus? They are all brought to a bad end, and the prized vineyard is left to others. That's us. We are the inheritors of the new promise. We harvest what Israel did not. It's as simple as that, we think. But if we stop there, the gospel will never strike us. We simply avoid its force.

One of the great virtues of the Hebrew scriptures and those who conscientiously read them is that such an easy way out is never taken. The Jews not only recorded the bad news prophets brought; they remembered it and relived it in the telling. That is what Jesus was doing. And that is what we are called to do if we wish to encounter the Word of God.

The parable of the vineyard, in both Isaiah's account and Jesus' reformulation of it for his contemporaries, must in some way be a message given to today's church. Although we believe in Jesus' promise that the armies of hell will not prevail against us, that should not lead us to think that we ourselves cannot squander the gift of the vineyard.

The "always reforming" church must always ask itself whether it seizes the vineyard inheritance for itself, rather than for the Lord of the harvest. It is only at great peril to themselves that the preacher, the mediator, and the institution, present themselves, rather than the Savior-Son, as the way of salvation. We put our very stewardship at risk if we follow a gospel other than that of Jesus.

Those who warn us that we neglect the ways of justice and close our ears to the cries of the poor are simply reminding us of the very gospel we proclaim. Those young people who wonder whether we stewards of the gospel are actually living as if the gospels didn't exist are not posing the question from a "worldly" perspective. They are posing it because they have received the seed of God's word and long to bear its fruit.

Isaiah promised that there would remain with God's people,

despite many infidelities, a "holy remnant" of faithful followers who carry the truth, cherish the message, and steadfastly
tend the vineyard. This remnant, I think at times, may be the
saints or the "little" people—those who aspire to no human
greatness, fabulous wealth, rank, or privilege. Perhaps it is they
who, even in these hard days when many Christians seem to
reject Christ as the rock of their lives, continue to build on
him as their cornerstone.

50. Dressed for the Banquet

Is. 25:6–10; Phil. 4:12–14, 19–20; Mt. 22:1–14

"The invited are many, the elect are few."

On God's mountain all people are given a banquet of rich food
and fine, aged wine. Mourning and death cease, and every tear
is wiped away. Shame is dispelled; hunger is forgotten. "This is
our God, in whom we hoped for salvation." Thus Isaiah recalls
the lush image of the banquet, that same feast of which the
psalmist sang, with food prepared in abundance, cups running
over, heads anointed with oil. It is the banquet of God that,
despite transient appetites or hungers, allows Paul to be satis-
fied no matter what his need or desire. "In him who is the
source of my strength I have strength for everything."

In the context of heaven's feast, the Gospel of Matthew
presents a strange story, one among many instances, actual or
symbolic, of dinners and banquets. In this particular case,
some of the invited are uninterested in the banquet prepared
for them. Others make light of it and go about their business;
still others ridicule and abuse those who bring the offer. So the
king sends his wards out into the streets to invite everyone,
good and bad alike, into the banquet. Eventually, however, the

king spots a visitor who is not wearing a robe, and the poor bloke is cast into darkness.

This has never been a very attractive story for me. It seems somewhat mercurial and vindictive. Why invite people to the banquet if you are going to reject them? Were not all called and welcome?

It is understandable that those who absolutely reject Christ and the bounty of his saving banquet are not included. They do not even want to come to the party. But the rest—all those who do not resist the possibility that God calls them to the eternal feast—are welcomed.

So why are some people who are already in the promised banquet-land excluded for the feeble-sounding reason that they are improperly dressed?

What has helped me understand this odd state of affairs is C. S. Lewis's wonderful fantasy, *The Great Divorce,* which he wrote to suggest that the option between heaven and hell is a radical choice we all have.

In this short, allegorical story, it turns out that a group of people, after a long bus ride, find themselves in a strange location. It is the vestibule of heaven itself, a place they have all generally wanted to go. The problem is that they must now believe that they are actually there. They must accept the fact that God really saves them.

Lewis develops a lively drama for each traveler's life. All they need to do is "put on" the armor of salvation to receive it; yet many of them cannot bring themselves to believe that they are in banquet-land. They would rather cling to the defenses with which they have covered themselves during their lives. One self-pitying chap, unwilling to let go of the mantle of his own righteousness, just cannot bring himself to trust that he is actually within the gates of Paradise. He grips his resentments so tightly that he disappears into the small dark hole of his egotism.

Another poor soul wears a small, slimy red lizard on his shoulder, a twitching, chiding garment of shame and disappointment. This lizard is his clothing, his self-image and self-presentation to the world. It is a symbol, Lewis leads us to believe, of some sin of lust, which the pilgrim soul both hugs for identity and carries for self-pity.

An angel approaches, offering to kill the slimy creature, which protests that if he is killed, the soul will surely lose his life and meaning. The ghost-soul, encouraged by the angel, finally lets go of the lizard, but only with trembling fear. He gasps out a final act of trust: "God help me. God help me."

And with that plea, a mortal struggle ensues, the lizard mightily resisting while a wondrous metamorphosis happens. The lizard is transformed into a glorious creature. "What stood before me was the greatest stallion I have ever seen, silvery white, but with mane and tail of gold. . . . The new-made man turned and clapped the new horse's neck. . . . In joyous haste the young man leaped upon the horse's back. Turning in his seat he waved a farewell, then nudged the stallion with his heels." They both soar off, like shooting stars, into the mountains and sunset.

What happened to this wayfarer at the vestibule of the banquet is that he finally clothed himself in Christ rather than in his shame. Having nothing of his own, not even his sins to cling to, he abandoned himself in the "God help me" of radical trust.

If it is God's will that we all be saved in Jesus, then it is for us, clothed in faith, hope, and love, to accept God's will as our own. Perhaps this is the meaning of Jesus' parable, as well as of Lewis's.

Paul wrote in his Letter to the Galatians that if we are baptized in Christ, we must be clothed in him. He is the only adequate banquet garment. And it is his love, we read in the Letter to the Colossians, that must be the clothing to complete and unify all others we wear. Yes, every child of the earth is called to the feast. But if any of us actually get there, it will only be because we are "all decked out" with Christ, in God.

51. To Caesar What Is God's

Is. 45:4–6; 1 Thess. 1:1–5; Mt. 22:15–21

"I am the Lord, there is no other."

It is fitting that the gospel readings in October and November frequently focus on radical discipleship. Late fall in the United States is, after all, the time of political choices, a season of elections, partisanship, and rival loyalties. In this season, it is hard to escape the political implications of the story of Jesus and Caesar's coin.

Of course the situation of Jesus, as well as of the community that collected the accounts of his life, differs vastly from our own. The gospel confrontation most likely represents a struggle between the party of Herod, loyal to Rome, and the Zealots, who refused tribute. Jesus seems to reject the Zealot contention, but he also distances himself from the Herodians.

The story is not simply about competing jurisdictions of church and state, nor about the isolated question of paying taxes (although both issues seem germane to our political campaigns as the century turns).

The taxation incident is one of five confrontations concerning the authority of Jesus. There are surrounding controversies over the acceptance of John the Baptist, over marriage, over the resurrection of the dead, over the great commandment, and over claims of messiahship.

In this particular conflict, we see Jesus confronted by a group of people who want to trip him up and undercut his mission, since they suspect that his parables are actually challenges to their power. His opponents use friendly, even smarmy words: "Dear teacher, truthful man, sincere fellow, you court no favor, nor ever act out of human respect." Then, aware of the hidden agenda in their question, whether it is lawful to pay taxes to the emperor, Jesus says that they should give the coin to the one whose face appears on it. "And give to God the things that are God's."

This scenario is particularly interesting if it is taken as a metaphor for conflicting loyalties in a "Judeo-Christian nation" as it faces the 1996 election at our century's wane. Both prominent antagonists and their handlers say the right words. They are all on the side of angels: family, values, truth, fairness, virtue, faith, blah blah blah. But the hidden agenda is really a question of authority. Who or what speaks to us authoritatively? I propose that it is not the choice between two political parties that pulls us one way or the other. (They are both pulling the same way: toward the empire of money, nationalism, and entertainment.) It is really a choice between Caesar and God.

What are we asked today to give to the empire? Is it our faith and moral practice? Our hopes and dreams? Our consciences? Our labor? Our children? And if we offer such sacrifices upon the altar of Caesar, have we betrayed the goods that are most intimately ours and God's?

The empire and those who vie for its throne offer us, in differing forms, an ideology of self-interest. One version of this promises us lower taxes and more prosperity, national security and power, enlightened egotism, and the narcissistic myth that since we have "earned" our possessions, the poor of our country and of the world can make no claim on us. The other version appeals to unbounded self-indulgence. Here we find individualistic choice exalted over every value and objective good imaginable. The clap-trap of rights talk, for example, has little to do with the intrinsic value of persons who command our respect by their very humanity. It is rather the scream of special interests grabbing attention, demanding satisfaction.

Out of both sides of the empire's mouth come sophistries. One jabbers about "morality," the other about "the right thing." But behind the glib words is a message: how good we have it, how much better off we will be if we vote for the privileged candidate.

In this political campaign precious few words will appeal to our generosity, our discipline, or our spirit of sacrifice. If there is talk of discipline and sacrifice, these will be prescribed for the poor. If there is language of compassion, it will ring of self-righteous narcissism.

The shroud of death haunting hospitals and refugee camps will not be mentioned. The deceptions of our official instruments of war and governance will not be uncovered. The voracious economy, which demands full-time work from both parents hoping to raise children, will not be addressed. The extravagant mountains of money for jaded entertainers and corporate merchants will not be brought up to embarrass us. We will only hear of what matters most: the products of our hands and the imaginings of our minds to which we supposedly turn for comfort and meaning, even salvation.

Isaiah's God was heard to say, "There is no God beside me." The Spirit that St. Paul preached led not to fatuous words but to active power. And Jesus knew what ought to be rendered to God: not lip-service, but heart and mind.

If we go to that polling place and vote for one of those who would lead us, let us do so well and judiciously. Give to Caesar.

But let us keep vigilance over our souls.

52. All You Need Is Love

Ex. 22:20–28; 1 Thess. 1:5–10; Mt. 22: 34–40

"The greatest commandment."

Love. What verb does more work? What noun is more invoked? That's the problem. The word "love" means too much and too little.

It stands for (and justifies) just about everything: strong desires, imperial needs, an obsessive ache, murder, atrocity, mendacity. People have done things for the "love" of God that God assuredly disavows. They have done things for love of others that have crushed the very objects of their obsession. They have done things for self-love that destroyed their very souls. Thus, the appeal to love is often not only trivial, it can be lethal.

I think there is no more misunderstood word than love. It means sex to some. Thrill to others. Feeling wonderful to most. Love should fix things, change them, renew them. It ought to make us feel better about ourselves and the world. It must make life light and easy, a joy, an ecstasy, bliss. As the song says, "Love is all you need."

Imagine the embarrassment and confusion then, when such a word, in the ironic play of God and the transcripts of history, shows up as the summation of the law and the prophets.

Yes, Jesus said it. He was responding to a question posed by a lawyer, of all people, who was wondering which commandment of the law was the greatest. His response? "You shall love the Lord your God with your whole heart, with your whole soul and with all your mind. This is the greatest and first commandment. The second is like it: You shall love your neighbor as yourself."

Now at first sight this answer was not earthshaking in its originality. The great Shema, a prayer that devout Jews recite every morning and night, is straight from the Book of Deuteronomy (6:5). This command to love God absolutely was to be "written on the heart" and drilled into the memory of every child. Mary, we may suppose, did her job.

The second part of the answer—"You must love your neighbor as yourself"—is lifted from Leviticus (19:18). What might have raised some eyebrows is that Jesus puts both of these commands on equal footing. The second is just like the first: our love of neighbor mirrors our love of God. Jesus, mind you, was not asked for two great laws, but he gave two as one. The entire will of God and purpose of our life is to love God with our whole being and our neighbors as ourselves.

So we're back to love, that chameleon that hides in the hue of everything and disappears into any context available.

But not so fast. This love isn't just anything. It involves heart and will, soul and life, mind and strength. It requires a covenantal fidelity. It makes demands. Love is not mere ardor; it is arduous.

The ordinances from the Book of Exodus are explicit enough on how love is exercised in human relations. We shall not wrong a resident alien. (Get that.) We shall not abuse widows or orphans. If we do, God's wrath will be upon us. If we lend money to the poor, we must not treat them as creditors or exact interest from them. (Now it is getting a little uncomfortable.) If we take anything as collateral that a neighbor needs, we must return it before the sun goes down. (So much for sweet romanticism.)

With Jesus, love is even more irksome. Not only does he identify love of neighbor with our love of ourselves and of God; he makes it quite clear that love is serving others, even laying down our lives for them.

Anyone who thinks that love is an easy path should consult the "more excellent way" of Paul's First Letter to the Corinthians. It is a passage, often heard at weddings, that could profitably be read every day and night of married life.

What is love? Love is patience. It is kindness. It is not jealous or conceited, rude or selfish. It does not take offense, nor is it resentful. It is always ready to trust, to excuse, and to endure whatever comes.

Love, when we do it, is the eternal in us, what lasts of us. It is God, again made flesh, in our reciprocation, our giving back. Love is ultimately an affirmation, a kiss to the universe freely given. True love is the wedding of faith and justice, the bond of transcendence with time. The love of God in whom we move and have our being is the same love made timely by our earthly care.

One day I received a note from someone who communicated a love to me that I found indubitable. She loved God first and, in God, all neighbors, herself, and even me. It was splendid and invincible. Although the gospel of Jesus inspired her, the words of Martin Buber expressed for her the holy mystery:

> Feelings accompany the metaphysical and metapsychical fact of love, but they do not constitute it. The accompanying feelings can be of greatly differing kinds. The feeling of Jesus for the demoniac differs from his feeling for the beloved disciple; but the love is the one love. Feelings are "entertained," love comes to pass. Feelings dwell in us; but we dwell in love. That is no metaphor, but the actual truth. In helping, healing, education, raising up, saving, love is the responsibility of an I for a Thou. In this lies the likeness—impossible in any feeling whatsoever—of all who love, from the smallest to the greatest and from the blessedly protected man, whose life is rounded in that of a loved being, to him who is all his life nailed to the cross of the world, and who ventures to bring himself to the dreadful point—to love all.

THIRTY-FIRST SUNDAY IN ORDINARY TIME

53. A Teaching Father

Mal. 1:14–2:2; 1 Thess. 2:7–9,13; Mt. 23:1–12

"Avoid the title."

Ever since my ordination I have been a little uncomfortable with Jesus' words about certain persons who are identified in Matthew's Gospel as scribes and Pharisees. "Do what they tell you," Jesus says, "but do not follow their example." They talk the talk, but they do not walk the walk. In fact, they bind up other people with impossible burdens, and they will not lift a finger to help them. These are the people who work in the limelight where their performances can be seen. They eagerly bear the marks of prestige, obtain the place of honor at banquets, take the front seats in church, and seek public respect.

This is hard-hitting stuff, especially if you sit up front every Sunday and now and then can be found ensconced at the head table. But what really lands a punch on the chin are Jesus' following words: "As for you, avoid the title 'Rabbi.' Only one among you is your teacher, the rest are learners. Do not call anyone on earth your father. Only one is your father, the one in heaven. Avoid being called teachers. One is your teacher, the Messiah."

Well, at least I'm not a rabbi. But people do call me teacher. I'm addressed as "Father" Kavanaugh. And sometimes I have at least acted as if I am the messiah. When I take the lower place at dinner, I wouldn't mind if someone came up and said, "Friend, go up higher." And if I've ever "humbled" myself, I suspect that the words "whoever humbles himself shall be exalted," lurked somewhere in the closets of my mind.

This business of titles and prestige bothers me. Since I first seriously read the Gospel of Matthew the year before I was ordained, I have always been a little sheepish, not shep- herdish, when people call me "Father"—even though I had looked forward to the title.

It's easy enough to ask handball players not to call me "Father" on the handball court. Even my partners feel a little strange when, at those increasingly rare moments, they shout, "Great kill, Father."

But the formal occasions are trickier. I'll never forget the time when I was to appear on a panel about ethics in America. It was going to be aired nationally, and there were a few big names seated in padded chairs around a big table. A man came around to get our official titles. I thought he might be Jewish, and I remembered a friend of mine who once told me that some Jews do not like to call a Catholic priest "Father." Even more to my discomfort, I was reminded of today's gospel passage, when he asked me, "What do you want me to call you? Father? Professor? Teacher?"

I went blank. "Call me anything you want. I'm a Catholic priest, a Jesuit at Saint Louis University. 'Brother' is a nice term—although I'm not officially a brother."

Eventually, the program started; and after a few initial probes to the panel, the moderator (Jack Ford, as I recall) said, "Mr. Kavanaugh, what do you think of this problem of privacy and the news media?"

Nobody answered. Then I realized he was talking to me. I hadn't been called "Mister" for such a long time I had forgotten what it sounded like. I suddenly felt untitled and ordinary. Others on the panel were chief executives or chief other things. Some were directors. A few were notables. I was just a mister.

To make matters worse, after the program aired, I received a letter from a bishop who was disappointed that I seemed to be covering up the fact I was a Catholic priest (though I was decked in black from head to toe).

I was never able to explain myself adequately to the bishop. I don't know if I can do so now. It's just that I'm a little queasy about being called "Father" or "teacher," even though I'm both, at least in some sense.

You, dear reader, need not bear the burden of my gospel literal-mindedness or my scruples, but it is noteworthy that Jesus makes such a big deal out of the whole thing.

Clearly he is talking about the danger of putting anyone in the place of God. Surely he is warning us against the tendency to set up a guru or a master as a solution for life's travails. And there is no doubt that Jesus is reminding all of us that we should not pose as the savior or master of anybody.

Only God is God. As St. Paul reminds the Thessalonians, our message, our word, and our teaching are God's, who works through and in us all. It is so tempting to make oneself the message and the teaching—especially if you have an honorific title.

If we wish honor or pre-eminence, let it be in service, rather than in being served. If we aspire to be Number One, let us be the first to forgive, to heal, to minister. We can't escape the message. Jesus is getting at something here.

We are brothers and sisters. That's that. In this matter of grace and salvation, there is no one of us above the other, even though some of us, by the grace of God, are asked to read the book, preach the word, offer the consecration, or pray the absolution. Our ministry, like St. Paul's, must be one of gentle encouragement, "as a mother," he says, sharing the Good News and graces of our lives. This may not make us look very imposing. But it will make us, with Paul, more grateful.

54. Postponement

Wis. 6:12–16; 1 Thess. 4:13–17; Mt. 25:1–13

"You do not know the hour."

Wisdom is unfading in splendor. She is found if she is sought. We must watch for her at dawn. "Whoever for her sake keeps vigils shall quickly be free from care." Wisdom makes her rounds, gracious and solicitous.

What is Wisdom that we might learn from her? We all look for sound judgment and keen insight. We seek depth of mind for an anchor. We await days when, free of illusion and pretense, we will see things as they really are and discern the gifts worth cherishing.

Everybody values, but few value what is valuable. Wisdom

is not so much knowing what one values as it is valuing something that is worthy of our care. We celebrate choice, but choices are a dime a dozen. What is rare is the wise choice.

As we approach the last few days, months, and years of this millennium, voices will be raised, as if inspired by wisdom, announcing the "end times." Readings from the gospels or letters like today's to the Thessalonians will be hauled out to predict the parousia, once again. Ears will perk up, expectant for God's trumpet and the archangel's call. There will be voices of prediction and perdition. Magazines will run articles on the Book of Revelation. Talk shows will chatter about the "rapture." Most of it will be clap-trap, little of it wise.

We have a gospel. It portrays ten bridesmaids, five of them foolish, five wise. The foolish ones have brought no oil reserve for their lamps, in case the first allotment runs out. The groom is late. Finally, he appears at midnight. The unprepared call out to the others, "Give us some oil." But the provident tell the foolish to get their own. And so the chance is missed, the door barred, even as those left behind cry for opening. It is too late. The moral of the story: "Keep your eyes open, for you know not the day or the hour."

There's the wisdom. We never know the hour or the day. All ten bridesmaids, recall, were asleep. The difference was that five of them were prepared. The point is not that we should calculate when destiny might arrive. It is that we should be ready for it every moment of our lives.

Readings that deal with the "end times" are not prognostications of the future, even though, with the church's year-end apocalyptic texts, we are reminded of the "four last things." That can be instructive, yes; but it is far wiser to think of the things that last. It is a mistake to take such passages as occult predictions concerning the end of the world. It is far wiser to see them as a way to wisdom at the start of each day. Each day may be our last. The farewell we give might never be given again. We may not see another day. To be wise, then, is not to calculate the time of departure. It is to spend the present moment—the waiting—well.

We rush through time to get things done. When we are not getting things done, we think we are wasting time. But the real waste of time is the way we rush through it. We may think we are active, but we are really inattentive. In hurrying to prepare ourselves for things not yet upon us, we are unprepared for what is here. And sooner or later, our gas runs out.

Almost ten years ago I made what I later thought was a foolish commitment. In a rash moment I volunteered to spend a year in Africa. Regretting my big mouth during the days following, this journey seemed to be the last thing I should do in my mid-forties, especially since I had so many other things to do, promises to keep, deadlines to make.

I had imagined myself vigilant and alert, so busy about the things of God and earth that I could barely keep up with life. A feeling of being "always rushed" had beset me. I began to resent the friends or students who would come to my door for talk, since they were taking up my time. (This was an ironic paradox: all I ever wanted was to "help" and be with people, the very gift that was getting on my nerves.)

I remember on the long trip, first to Australia and then over an endless sea to the coast of Africa, how I rued that impetuous act of volunteering. I had so much to do. And here I was letting a year of my life disappear in a village on the edge of Harare, Zimbabwe.

It took about a month for gracious and solicitous Wisdom to show her face. After weeks of quiet walks, gentle and unrushed conversations with Shona and Ndebele, fewer compulsions to keep up with news, sports, weather, and all the ephemeral opinion columns I daily consumed, Wisdom made her rounds to me—not when I was watching for her at dawn, but at the moment of a day's dusk.

Sitting on a porch overlooking a valley unknown to and unmentioned by almost everyone in history, I beheld the meaning of a day. Freed, for a moment, by Wisdom from my cares, I felt the end times.

It was all opportunity. It is all now. The last things are the lasting things: this moment of gratitude, this one gift of another breath, this particular person before me, this chance to hope, this hour to believe. It is all now. Eternity is now. And God is with us. All that we need is to be alert. At life's end, no matter what the hour or day, we will only welcome the presence to whom, in our rare wise times, we have learned to be attentive.

55. Stewardship

Prov. 31:10–13, 19–20, 30–31; 1 Thess. 5:1–6;
Mt. 24:36, 25:14–30

"Out of fear, I buried it."

The parable of the talents tells a tale of three servants who are entrusted with funds in varying quantities in proportion to their abilities—five, two, and one. The first servant invested everything to yield another five. The one with two talents doubled the sum. A third, given one talent, dug a hole and buried it. When the master returned, he rewarded those who doubled their resources, commending their trustworthiness: "Come, share your master's joy."

But the servant who buried the talent gave a different report of stewardship: "I know you are a hard man, so out of fear I went off and buried your talent in the ground. Here is your money back."

For this he is called a worthless, lazy lout. "You should have banked it and got interest." After the sum is given to the others, and just before the laggard is thrown out into the dark to grind his teeth, the master says, "Those who have will get more until they grow rich, while those who have not will lose even the little they have."

It is no shock that the parable of the talents is often taken as a recommendation of usury and capitalism. Even the *Jerome Biblical Commentary* seems to suggest as much. In the 1980s, as if in response to the U.S. Catholic bishops' pastoral on the economy, the Lay Commission on Catholic Social Teaching and the U.S. Economy wrote a "letter" of its own, which featured the parable. This document noted that while the parable of the wise and foolish virgins shows that "good intentions are not enough," and the last judgment story reminds us to care for the poor and needy, this parable of the talents describes the "terrible punishments which lie in store for those who do not produce new wealth from the talents God has placed in their stewardship." The parable of talents, we are told, helps us understand the "moral élan" of the U.S. economy.

While the commission's letter is a thoughtful effort at integrating capitalism with the demands of the gospel, I think the parable of the talents has as little to do with capitalism as it does with slavery or absolute control over the destiny of the servants who appear as characters in the story.

The three parables in the twenty-fifth chapter of Matthew are about the end times, the end of the world, the end (intent, purpose, and upshot) of our lives. Whatever is given to us— money, talent, opportunity—is meant to bear fruit for the kingdom, for the glory of God and the salvation of souls. As the parable immediately following the one about the talents makes clear, the entire judgment of history and of each individual is based upon our service to the least of our brothers and sisters.

In its most fundamental sense, the image of the talent represents the bounty of life itself, as well as the pre-eminent gift of faith. If we are among those fortunate enough to reach the maturity required for personal responsibility and to have the opportunity to use the talents of life and faith, it is incumbent upon us to invest our gifts, not hide them out of fear or laziness.

The parable is not about the stock market or entrepreneurship, commendable as those activities might be. It is about what we do with our gifts, financial or otherwise.

If anyone thinks that amassing wealth is somehow a good in itself (and I do not believe the writers of the Lay Commission's letter do), that person is seriously mistaken. Do not take it from me, but from the twelfth chapter of Luke: "Be on your guard against all kinds of greed; for one's life does not consist in abundance of possessions." After Jesus issues this warning, he tells another story of a rich man whose land produced abundantly. What he did was to build larger storehouses for his goods, saying to himself, "Soul, you have ample goods laid up for many years; relax, eat, drink, be merry." God calls such people fools, since they store up treasures for themselves but are not rich in the sight of God.

I do not think that one can find either a recommendation or a rejection of capitalism in the gospels, although it is quite clear that the amassing of money for oneself is considered not only foolish, but evil. There are more warnings in the gospels about the dangers of money than about any other earthly good, so a successful Catholic capitalist is well advised to be most vigilant in stewardship. The goods of the world and the wealth derived from our labor must be used for God's glory and human assistance. What is more, if a Christian would defend the benefits of capitalism, it ought to be based on the argument that capitalism is most effective in the service of God and ministry to the poor, homeless, and hungry.

The trustworthiness of the profitable servants ensures their share in the "joy of the Lord." This is not because money is made. It is, rather, because the wealth of life and talent given them had been invested to bear fruit in labors of faith, hope, and charity.

Whether we are millionaires or paupers, it is upon this criterion that we will be judged.

56. The Gospel Realm

Ez. 34:11–12, 15–17; 1 Cor. 15:20–28; Mt. 25:31–46

"When did we see you?"

Matthew's great parable of the last judgment presents the glorified Son of Man, with an entourage of angels, rising before the nations of the world. The blessed and lost are separated by one norm: the care of others. "Inherit the kingdom prepared for you from the creation of the world. For I was hungry and you gave me food, I was thirsty and you gave me drink. I was a stranger and you welcomed me, naked and you clothed me. I was ill and you comforted me, in prison and you came to visit me."

This proclamation is formulated four times in the course of the parable. It is worth the four repetitions. For, like many gospel passages, we have heard the words so often that they seem ordinary, even though they are the most revolutionary claims about the human condition that have ever been made.

In all the ways that God has been revealed to high human consciousness, there has been one abiding theme: the dignity and value of the human person. The ancient Chinese may have been among the first to formulate it: never do to others what you would not have done to yourself. Archaic Babylonian law commanded that we show good will to others. The mighty Egyptians were told, "Terrorize not a human." Buddha reached enlightenment only when he embarked on the life of compassion for others. And Jewish faith, parent of both Christianity and Islam, revealed the source of the truth: "Male and female God created them; in God's own image were they created."

For Christians, this revelation of God reached its apex in the Incarnation: the Word of God became human flesh to save us. Thus it is strategic that Matthew, immediately before the narrative of Jesus' passion and death, presents the scene of the last judgment as a metaphor wherein the least human person is identified with the Lord of history.

On one level of interpretation, this parable is an indictment of humanity's violent resistance to God's revelation. In our own century millions have been killed in the Middle East for the sake of homeland and nation. Eleven million Hindus and Muslims were slaughtered at the dawn of India's freedom. Twenty million were purged in Communist China. The killing fields of Cambodia were marked by a million skulls. Rwanda and Serbia still sink under waves of blood.

Before our own times entire tribes of indigenous peoples disappeared in North and South America, sacrificed to idols of gold. Jews were banished or forcibly converted long before the abominable "final solution." Holy "religious" wars were launched in the name of God. Children of every color and tribe have been traded or killed upon birth.

To such a bleak history, the Lord of history has spoken: "As often as you have done this to the least of my brothers and sisters, you have done it to me."

Like all of holy scripture, the parable of the end times is a judgment on the world. In human mayhem, we dismember the body of Christ. "You have done it to me." The starving, the unwanted old and unborn, the criminal, the enemy—"the least"—are him.

This judgment of God is a moral command as well. In the eyes of Christ's followers, the bodies of the wounded and murdered are bodies of Christ. Thus, killing is sacrilege. All wars are unholy. Any "choice" to kill a human being is an ungodly act.

But the story is more radical yet. For the parable not only judges history. It calls us to active love. It is an invitation to see Christ in each other. In all our relations we encounter God. Spouses, children, neighbors all count as "the least." Every wife who comforted her husband, every father who gave joy to his child, every friend who consoled a companion, every mother who fed the infant or held the dying has encountered the Lord.

We all bear the presence of the Most High, no matter how diminished or devalued we may seem. We are bodies of Christ. Every reception of holy Communion reaffirms the truth: Christ assumes our flesh as his own.

Scripture, in its greatest depth, does not merely present a moral challenge or a judgment on the world. Nor is it a program for political or social action, or a self-help book. It is, rather, a story of the mystery of salvation.

For at the end of history, Jesus Christ, the Word of God made human flesh, addresses also the one who sent him: "Whatsoever you do to the least of my brothers and sisters, you do unto me." These words that challenge us are the very words that save us.

What if, in our thinking, our praying, and our writing about scripture, we accepted it as if it were real? What if the Word of God is actually true on all levels of our lives—true for a world of nations, politics, or economies; true for our relations with each other; true for each of us in our hearts; true of God?

If you and I accept, with all our mind and will, the promise of God's Word, perhaps then we shall fully understand the soaring words of Paul: "Christ must reign until God has put all enemies under his feet, and the last enemy to be destroyed is death."